Horatio N. Robinson, Daniel W. Fish

Robinson's Progressive Intellectual Arithmetic

on the inductive plan: being a sequel to the Progressive primary arithmetic

Horatio N. Robinson, Daniel W. Fish

Robinson's Progressive Intellectual Arithmetic
on the inductive plan: being a sequel to the Progressive primary arithmetic

ISBN/EAN: 9783337882297

Printed in Europe, USA, Canada, Australia, Japan

Cover: Foto ©Andreas Hilbeck / pixelio.de

More available books at **www.hansebooks.com**

ROBINSON'S

PROGRESSIVE

INTELLECTUAL ARITHMETIC;

ON THE INDUCTIVE PLAN.

BEING

A SEQUEL TO THE PROGRESSIVE PRIMARY ARITHMETIC, CONTAINING
MANY ORIGINAL FORMS OF ANALYSIS APPLICABLE TO A
GREAT VARIETY OF PRACTICAL QUESTIONS,

AND DESIGNED FOR

THE MORE ADVANCED CLASSES

IN

COMMON SCHOOLS AND ACADEMIES.

EDITED BY

DANIEL W. FISH, A.M.

IVISON, BLAKEMAN, TAYLOR & CO.,
PUBLISHERS,
NEW YORK AND CHICAGO.
1878.

ROBINSON'S
Mathematical Series.

Graded to the wants of Primary, Intermediate, Grammar,
Normal, and High Schools, Academies, and Colleges.

Progressive Table Book.
Progressive Primary Arithmetic.
Progressive Intellectual Arithmetic.
Rudiments of Written Arithmetic.
JUNIOR-CLASS ARITHMETIC, Oral and Written. NEW.
Progressive Practical Arithmetic.
Key to Practical Arithmetic.
Progressive Higher Arithmetic.
Key to Higher Arithmetic.
New Elementary Algebra.
Key to New Elementary Algebra.
New University Algebra.
Key to New University Algebra.
New Geometry and Trigonometry. In one vol.
Geometry, Plane and Solid. In separate vol.
Trigonometry, Plane and Spherical. In separate vol.
New Analytical Geometry and Conic Sectio
New Surveying and Navigation.
New Differential and Integral Calculus.
University Astronomy— Descriptive and Physical.
Key to Geometry and Trigonometry, Analytical Geometry and Conic Sec-
tions, Surveying and Navigation.

Entered, according to Act of Congress, in the year 1858, and again in the year 1863, by

DANIEL W. FISH, A.M.,

In the Clerk's Office of the District Court of the United States, for the Northern
District of New York.

PREFACE.

THE importance, and the practical benefit to be derived from the study of Intellectual Arithmetic, not only as a preparation for business life, but as a means of developing and strengthening the thinking and reasoning powers, and of *thorough mental* culture, can not be over-estimated. Not only is it a necessary study for *young* pupils, but indispensable to the more advanced student, as a preparation for the prompt and accurate business man. And it is believed that, as a general rule, the most *critical, correct,* and *ready* students of mathematics are those who have been most thoroughly drilled in intellectual arithmetic.

This work has been prepared more especially for *advanced* classes, and is designed for those who have first been well taught in the primary book, and for such as are pursuing the study of written arithmetic, or algebra, and who have never been *thoroughly* exercised in this branch of study.

Only a few of the many points of difference between this and other similar works, and which, it is believed, renders this superior to them, will be referred to.

It is more *complete, comprehensive,* and *progressive* in its character. The arrangement and classification are more strictly *systematic,* and in accordance with the natural order of mathematical science. The development of principles, and their applications, are shown by a more numerous selection, and greater variety of appropriate examples, *progressively* arranged, commencing with those that are simple and easy, and advancing to those more complex and difficult.

At intervals, and especially in the closing sections of each chapter, examples are given containing such a combination of principles, and forms of analysis, as to require a knowledge of almost every principle *previously* taught, thus affording the pupil a thorough review, as well as requiring him to *classify* his knowledge of what he has been over.

One of the most important, and, it is thought, one of the most original and useful features of this work, is the *full, concise,* and *uniform* system of ANALYSIS it contains, — the result of long experience in the school-room.

Particular attention is invited to the subjects of *Fractions, Percentage,* and *Interest*; their treatment is peculiar, and adapted to obviate many of the difficulties, and greatly *abbreviate* most of the operations in them.

4 PREFACE.

The chapter of Miscellaneous Examples will afford a valuable
and thorough drill to the advanced student of arithmetic or algebra. They contain a great variety of principles, and while they
may be considered difficult, yet the full analysis given of every
principle, and the selection of numbers so adapted to the conditions
of the question as to produce results free from large and difficult
fractions, will render a *mental* solution of them comparatively easy.

In conclusion, we may be allowed to express the belief, that
in this work the thorough teacher will find a *desideratum* long
sought in this department of science,—the means of mental discipline and development such as has been furnished by no
similar treatise.

THE AUTHOR.

SUGGESTIONS TO TEACHERS.

Pupils of nearly the same degree of advancement should be
classed together. Regular exercises should be assigned to the
class, and sufficient time allowed them to thoroughly examine
their lesson before being called upon to recite.

The use of the book at the time of recitation should be *strictly
prohibited*, except, perhaps, in some of the more difficult lessons
in the latter part of the work.

Each example should be read but *once, slowly and distinctly*,
the pupils called upon *promiscuously*, who should arise, stand
erect, repeat the example, and then give the analysis. This will
secure close attention.

Every question should be *clearly and thoroughly analyzed*, and
the pupil required to adhere strictly to the *forms* of solution given,
unless better ones can be substituted; and in no case should he
be allowed to omit the *conclusion*, commencing with " Therefore."

The class should be encouraged to detect and correct errors in
statement or analysis, to criticise and make proper inquiries, all
of which should be signaled by the uplifted hand.

It is suggested that the class be occasionally exercised upon
" Ringing the Changes," as explained in the Appendix, and which
may be applied to a great number and variety of examples. It
will not only afford a valuable drill, but a pleasant and enlivening
exercise.

INTELLECTUAL ARITHMETIC.

CHAPTER I.

ADDITION.

1. 1. JAMES had 1 cent, and his father gave him 1 more ; how many had he then ?

2. If a slate pencil cost 2 cents, and a steel pen 1 cent, how many cents will both cost ?

3. George spent 2 cents for candy, and had 2 cents left ; how many cents had he at first ?

4. A farmer sold a calf for 3 dollars, and a pig for 2 dollars ; how many dollars did he receive for both ?

5. Mary gave 2 cents for some tape, and 5 cents for a thimble ; how many cents did she give for both ?

6. Martin gave John 3 apples, and kept 4 for himself ; how many apples had he at first ?

7. There are 4 books on one desk, and 2 books on another ; how many books on both desks ?

8. If a lemon cost 3 cents, and an orange 5 cents, how many cents do both cost ?

9. In a certain class there are 5 girls and 4 boys ; how many pupils in the class ?

10. Samuel had 3 marbles, and his brother gave him 3 more ; how many did he then have ?

11. Bought a barrel of apples for 2 dollars, and a cord of wood for 4 dollars ; how many dollars did both cost ?

1*

2.

1. 1 and 1 are how many ?
2. 1 and 2 are how many ?
3. 2 and 2 are how many ?
4. 2 and 3 are how many ?
5. 2 and 4 are how many ?
6. 2 and 5 are how many ?
7. 2 and 6 are how many ?
8. 2 and 7 are how many ?
9. 2 and 8 are how many ?
10. 2 and 9 are how many ?
11. 3 and 3 are how many ?
12. 3 and 4 are how many ?
13. 3 and 5 are how many ?
14. 3 and 6 are how many ?
15. 3 and 7 are how many ?
16. 3 and 8 are how many ?
17. 3 and 9 are how many ?
18. 3 and 10 are how many ?
19. 4 and 2 are how many ?
20. 4 and 3 are how many ?
21. 4 and 4 are how many ?
22. 4 and 5 are how many ?
23. 4 and 6 are how many ?
24. 4 and 7 are how many ?
25. 4 and 8 are how many ?
26. 4 and 9 are how many ?
27. 4 and 10 are how many ?
28. 5 and 1 are how many ?
29. 5 and 2 are how many ?
30. 5 and 3 are how many ?
31. 5 and 4 are how many ?
32. 5 and 5 are how many ?
33. 5 and 6 are how many ?
34. 5 and 7 are how many ?
35. 5 and 8 are how many ?
36. 5 and 9 are how many ?

3. 1. A man bought a calf for 7 dollars, and sold it for 3 dollars more than he gave for it; how much did he sell it for?

2. Bought a barrel of cider for 2 dollars, and 20 bushels of apples for 8 dollars; how many dollars did the whole cost?

3. If a coat cost 10 dollars, and a pair of pantaloons 5 dollars, what will be the cost of both?

4. A merchant bought 4 boxes of black tea, and 7 boxes of green tea; how many boxes did he buy of both kinds?

5. A farmer sold 5 sheep to one man, and 9 to another; how many did he sell to both?

6. Ralph walked 4 miles and rode 10 miles; how many miles did he go?

7. Philip answered 8 questions in geography, and Oliver 5; how many questions did both answer?

8. If a quart of chestnuts cost 10 cents, and a quart of walnuts 4 cents, what will be the cost of one quart of both?

9. 6 and 3 are how many?
10. 6 and 4 are how many?
11. 6 and 5 are how many?
12. 6 and 6 are how many?
13. 6 and 7 are how many?
14. 6 and 8 are how many?
15. 6 and 9 are how many?
16. 6 and 10 are how many?
17. 7 and 4 are how many?
18. 7 and 5 are how many?
19. 7 and 6 are how many?
20. 7 and 7 are how many?
21. 7 and 8 are how many?
22. 7 and 9 are how many?
23. 7 and 10 are how many?
24. 8 and 3 are how many?

25. 8 and 4 are how many?
26. 8 and 5 are how many?
27. 8 and 6 are how many?
28. 8 and 7 are how many?
29. 8 and 8 are how many?
30. 8 and 9 are how many?
31. 8 and 10 are how many?
32. 9 and 4 are how many?
33. 9 and 5 are how many?
34. 9 and 6 are how many?
35. 9 and 7 are how many?
36. 9 and 8 are how many?
37. 9 and 9 are how many?
38. 9 and 10 are how many?
39. 10 and 4 are how many?
40. 10 and 5 are how many?
41. 10 and 6 are how many?

---

4. 1. Eli paid 9 shillings for a pair of skates, and 6 shillings for a cap; how many shillings did he pay for both?

ANALYSIS. *Since Eli paid 9 shillings for a pair of skates, and 6 shillings for a cap, he paid for both, the sum of 9 shillings and 6 shillings. The sum of 9 shillings and 6 shillings is 15 shillings. Therefore, he paid 15 shillings for both.*

2. A farmer sold some oats for 7 dollars, and a ton of hay for 9 dollars; how many dollars did he receive for both?

3. Paid 8 cents for some raisins, and 6 cents for some cloves; how many cents did both cost?

4. Nancy is 10 years old; how old will she be 5 years from this time?

5. A lady paid 7 dollars for a

6. There are 9 boys in one class, and 7 in another; how many in both classes?

7. Margaret has 8 flower pots in one room, and 5 in another; how many has she in the two rooms?

8. If you read 10 pages to-day, and 7 pages to-morrow, how many will you read in both days?

9. If a firkin of butter is worth 9 dollars, and two cords of wood are worth 8 dollars, what are both worth?

10. Myron has 6 young rabbits and 4 old ones; how many rabbits has he?

11. There are 10 birds sitting on one limb, and 9 on another; how many birds on both limbs?

12. A boy, having some peaches given him, put 8 into his hat, and 7 into his pockets; how many peaches were given him?

13. Edwin found 6 ripe pears under one tree, and 8 under another; how many pears did he find under both trees?

14. In one yard are 5 cows, and in another 7; how many cows in both yards?

15. If you work 8 examples in arithmetic to-day, and 8 more to-morrow, how many will you work in both days?

16. Robert gave 8 nuts to Henry, and kept 9; how many nuts had he at first?

5.
1. 7 and 4 are how many?
2. 9 and 7 are how many?
3. 6 and 7 are how many?
4. 5 and 9 are how many?
5. 8 and 7 are how many?
6. 10 and 6 are how many?
7. 9 and 6 are how many?
8. 8 and 8 are how many?

9.   6 and 8   are how many?
10. 7 and 9   are how many?
11. 8 and 10   are how many?
12. 11 and 5   are how many?
13. 13 and 7   are how many?
14. 14 and 6   are how many?
15. 12 and 4   are how many?
16. 15 and 8   are how many?
17. 9 and 12   are how many?
18. 16 and 8   are how many?
19. 17 and 10   are how many?
20. 15 and 11   are how many?
21. 13 and 12   are how many?

22. How many are 2 and 2? 12 and 2? 22 and 2? 32 and 2? 42 and 2? 52 and 2? 62 and 2? 72 and 2? 82 and 2? 92 and 2?

23. How many are 3 and 3? 13 and 3? 23 and 3? 33 and 3? 43 and 3? 53 and 3? 63 and 3? 73 and 3? 83 and 3? 93 and 3?

24. How many are 4 and 4? 14 and 4? 24 and 4? 34 and 4? 44 and 4? 54 and 4? 64 and 4? 74 and 4? 84 and 4? 94 and 4?   .

25. How many are 5 and 5? 15 and 5? 25 and 5? 35 and 5? 45 and 5? 55 and 5? 65 and 5? 75 and 5? 85 and 5? 95 and 5?

26. How many are 6 and 6? 16 and 6? 26 and 6? 36 and 6? 46 and 6? 56 and 6? 66 and 6? 76 and 6? 86 and 6? 96 and 6?

27. How many are 7 and 7? 17 and 7? 27 and 7? 37 and 7? 47 and 7? 57 and 7? 67 and 7? 77 and 7? 87 and 7? 97 and 7?

28. How many are 8 and 8? 18 and 8? 28 and 8? 38 and 8? 48 and 8? 58 and 8? 68 and 8? 78 and 8? 88 and 8? 98 and 8?

29. How many are 9 and 9? 19 and 9? 29 and

30. How many are 8 and 7 ? 18 and 7 ? 28 and 7 ? 38 and 7 ? 48 and 7 ? 58 and 7 ? 68 and 7 ? 78 and 7 ? 88 and 7 ? 98 and 7 ?

31. How many are 10 and 10 ? 20 and 10 ? 30 and 10 ? 40 and 10 ? 50 and 10 ? 60 and 10 ? 70 and 10 ? 80 and 10 ? 90 and 10 ?

32. How many are 4 and 8 ? 14 and 8 ? 24 and 8 ? 34 and 8 ? 44 and 8 ? 54 and 8 ? 64 and 8 ? 74 and 8 ? 84 and 8 ? 94 and 8 ?

33. How many are 6 and 5 ? 16 and 5 ? 26 and 5 ? 36 and 5 ? 46 and 5 ? 56 and 5 ? 66 and 5 ? 76 and 5 ? 86 and 5 ? 96 and 5 ?

34. How many are 11 and 9 ? 21 and 9 ? 31 and 9 ? 41 and 9 ? 51 and 9 ? 61 and 9 ? 71 and 9 ? 81 and 9 ? 91 and 9 ?

35. How many are 9 and 7 ? 19 and 7 ? 29 and 7 ? 39 and 7 ? 49 and 7 ? 59 and 7 ? 69 and 7 ? 79 and 7 ? 89 and 7 ? 99 and 7 ?

36. How many are 4 and 8 ? 14 and 8 ? 24 and 8 ? 34 and 8 ? 44 and 8 ? 54 and 8 ? 64 and 8 ? 74 and 8 ? 84 and 8 ? 94 and 8 ?

37. How many are 3 and 10 ? 13 and 10 ? 23 and 10 ? 33 and 10 ? 43 and 10 ? 53 and 10 ? 63 and 10 ? 73 and 10 ? 83 and 10 ? 93 and 10 ?

———————

6. *Addition* is the process of uniting several numbers of the same kind into one equivalent number. The result is called the *Sum* or *Amount*. The sign of addition is written thus, $+$, and is called *plus*. When placed between two numbers or quantities, it shows that they are to be added together. Thus, $5 + 3 + 2$ signifies that 5 and 3 and 2 are to be added together, and is read *five, plus three, plus two.*

The sign of equality is written thus, $=$. When placed between two numbers or quantities, it signifies that the latter is *equal to* the former.

1.   6 + 4 + 5   are how many?
2.   9 + 7 + 3   are how many?
3.   10 + 6 + 4   are how many?
4.   13 + 8 + 6   are how many?
5.   12 + 10 + 9   are how many?
6.   11 + 6 + 7   are how many?
7.   8 + 10 + 7 + 6   are how many?
8.   34 + 25   are how many?

ANALYSIS. *As many as the sum of 34 and 25; 34 is composed of 3 tens and 4 units, and 25 of 2 tens and 5 units; 3 tens and 2 tens are 5 tens, or 50, and 4 units and 5 units are 9 units, which added to 50 makes 59. Therefore 34 + 25 are 59.*

 9.   46 + 31   are how many?
10.   35 + 52   are how many?
11.   40 + 30 + 6   are how many?
12.   19 + 12 + 8   are how many?
13.   60 + 72 + 4   are how many?
14.   48 + 30 + 10   are how many?
15.   13 + 25 + 7   are how many?
16.   29 + 24 + 30   are how many?
17.   64 + 40 + 9   are how many?
18.   29 + 17 + 12   are how many?
19.   7 + 37 + 26   are how many?
20.   14 + 39 + 4   are how many?
21.   48 + 31 + 9   are how many?
22.   56 + 41 + 10   are how many?
23.   75 + 60 + 20   are how many?
24.   16 + 19 + 28   are how many?
25.   43 + 37 + 15   are how many?
26.   84 + 75 + 20   are how many?
27.   68 + 52 + 45   are how many?
28.   35 + 77 + 51   are how many?
29.   80 + 95 + 12   are how many?
30.   42 + 38 + 17 + 9   are how many?

7. 1. A man gave 12 dollars for some corn, 8 dollars for a ton of hay, and 6 dollars for a barrel of flour ; how much did he pay for all ?

ANALYSIS. *He p.... the sum of 12 dollars, 8 dollars, and 6 dollars ; 12 and 8 are 20, and 6 are 26 dollars. Therefore, &c.*

2. Emily paid 12 shillings for a dress, 10 shillings for a pair of shoes, and 6 shillings for a pair of gloves ; what was the cost of the whole ?

3. A drover had 15 horses in one pasture, 13 in another, and 9 in another ; how many horses had he ?

4. James has 10 cents, Henry has 7, and John has 5 ; how many cents have the three boys?

5. Bought a pound of candles for 14 cents, a pound of coffee for 12 cents, and a bar of soap for 9 cents ; what was the cost of the whole ?

6. In a shop are 7 men, 9 boys, and 6 girls at work ; how many persons at work in the shop ?

7. A lady sold 10 pounds of butter at one time, 12 pounds at another, and 8 pounds at another; how many pounds did she sell in all ?

8. William bought an arithmetic for 15 cents, a quire of paper for 12 cents, and a bottle of ink for 6 cents ; what was the cost of the whole ?

9. Peter, Dexter, and Irwin gave some money to a beggar ; Peter gave him 10 cents, Dexter 11 cents, and Irwin 13 cents ; how many cents did they all give him ?

10. In a certain school there are 18 girls and 24 boys ; how many pupils in the school ?

11. A man bought a sleigh for 20 dollars, paid 10 dollars for repairing it, and 6 dollars for painting it ; what did it cost him ?

12. Morgan earned 25 cents one day, and 32 the next; how much did he earn in both days ?

13. A farmer sold a cow for 22 dollars, a ton of hay for 11 dollars, and a calf for 7 dollars; what did he receive for all ?

14. A traveler walked 3C miles one day, 26 miles the next, and 21 miles the next; how many miles did he travel in the three days ?

15. One day Sarah wrote 18 lines, Maria 16, and Carrie 15 ; how many lines did they all write ?

16. A man gave 60 dollars for a horse, 23 dollars for a saddle, and 9 dollars for a bridle ; what was the cost of the whole ?

17. Rollin received 36 new cents on his birthday, 34 on Christmas day, and 27 on New Year's day ; how many cents did he receive ?

18. A man bought a piece of land for 56 dollars, and paid 25 dollars for fencing it ; for how much must he sell it to gain 15 dollars ?

19. Amasa, going into the orchard, found 12 ripe apples under one tree, 15 under another, 11 under another, and 9 under another ; how many apples did he find under the four trees ?

20. A grocer bought some hams for 20 dollars, some oats for 19 dollars, some fowls for 16 dollars, and five barrels of apples for 10 dollars; what did he pay for all ?

21. A miller shipped by railroad 28 barrels of flour at one time, 37 at another, and 40 at another ; how many barrels did he ship ?

22. If Lucian gave 45 cents for a penknife, 15 cents for some paper, 12 cents for a folder, and 7 cents for some wafers, what did the whole cost him ?

23. A drover bought 26 sheep of one man, 30 of another, 37 of another, and 40 of another ; how many sheep did he purchase ?

24. Bought a horse for 75 dollars, and sold him so as to gain 25 dollars ; how much did I receive for him ?

25. A lady went shopping, and bought a silk dress, for 22 dollars, a muff for 16 dollars, a shawl for 14 dollars, and had 7 dollars left; how much money had she at first?

26. Peleg bought a knife for 35 cents; he gave the knife and 12 cents for a sled, which he sold so as to gain 10 cents on the cost; how much did he receive for the sled?

27. In a certain orchard are 31 apple trees, 27 peach trees, and 19 pear trees; how many trees in the orchard?

28. A farmer raised 54 bushels of wheat, 66 bushels of oats, and 40 bushels of corn; how many bushels of grain did he raise?

29. If it be 62 feet from the ground to the belfry of a church, and 76 feet from the belfry to the top of the steeple, how high is the top of the steeple from the ground?

30. In March are 31 days, in April 30, in May 31; how many days in those three months?

31. If a farm contain 83 acres of cleared land and 25 acres of wood land, how many acres are in the whole farm?

32. The distance from Boston to Worcester is 44 miles, from Worcester to Warren 29 miles, and from Warren to Springfield 25 miles; how many miles from Boston to Springfield?

33. Batavia is 37 miles west from Rochester, and 31 miles east from Buffalo by railroad; what is the distance from Rochester to Buffalo?

34. A tailor bought three pieces of cloth, the first containing 29 yards, the second 26 yards, and the third 25 yards; how many yards did the three pieces contain?

35. A mechanic sold a carriage for 15 dollars, and a sleigh for 48 dollars; what did he receive for both?

36. A soldier was 33 years of age when he engaged in the battle of New Orleans; what was his age 44 years after ?

37. A farmer received 29 dollars for some pork, 18 dollars for some hay, 15 dollars for some oats, and 12 dollars for four cords of wood; how many dollars did he receive for the whole ?

38. Thomas hoed 13 rows of corn, Lyman 16 rows, Cyrus 14 rows, and Warren 10 rows; how many rows did they all hoe ?

39. A gentleman gave 30 dollars for a coat, 7 dollars for a vest, 11 dollars for a pair of pantaloons, and 5 dollars for a hat; what was the cost of all ?

40. Paid 60 dollars for a carriage, which, with 25 dollars, I gave for a horse; paid 12 dollars for his keeping, and then sold him for 20 dollars more than he cost me; for how much did I sell him ?

41. A man deposited 40 dollars in a bank, which was 15 dollars less than his neighbor deposited at the same time; how much did both deposit ?

CHAPTER II.

SUBTRACTION.

8. 1. JAMES, having 5 cents, gave 2 cents for a pencil; how many cents had he left ?

ANALYSIS. *Since James had 5 cents, and gave 2 cents for a pencil, he had left the difference between 5 cents and 2 cents. The difference between 5 cents and 2 cents, is 3 cents. Therefore, he had 3 cents left.*

2. Mary had 3 peaches, and ate 1 of them; how many had she left ?

3. Ella had 6 pinks, and gave her sister 2; how many had she left ?

4. On a rose bush were 7 roses, and Eliza picked 3 of them; how many were left?

5. A man bought 10 sheep and sold 5 of them; how many had he left?

6. A bad boy robbed a bird's nest of 7 eggs, and broke 4 of them; how many remained unbroken?

7. If there are 8 pigs in a pen, and five of them get out, how many remain?

8. If a merchant have 12 barrels of flour, and he sell 7 of them, how many barrels will he have left?

9. Margaret is 11 years old, and Julia 4 years younger; what is Julia's age?

10. Stephen had 9 marbles, and lost 3 of them; how many had he left?

11. A man, earning 10 dollars a week, spends 6 dollars for provisions; how many dollars has he left?

12. Giles borrowed 12 dollars, and paid 7 dollars of it; how much of it remained unpaid?

13.	5	less	3	are how many?
14.	9	less	2	are how many?
15.	7	less	4	are how many?
16.	11	less	3	are how many?
17.	8	less	2	are how many?
18.	6	less	4	are how many?
19.	10	less	6	are how many?
20.	7	less	5	are how many?
21.	14	less	8	are how many?
22.	12	less	7	are how many?
23.	9	less	8	are how many?
24.	15	less	9	are how many?
25.	20	less	6	are how many?
26.	23	less	10	are how many?
27.	18	less	4	are how many?

2

28. 11 from 14 leaves how many?
29. 9 from 12 leaves how many?
30. 7 from 16 leaves how many?
31. 12 from 20 leaves how many?
32. 10 from 17 leaves how many?
33. 8 from 18 leaves how many?
34. 6 from 15 leaves how many?
35. 11 from 21 leaves how many?
36. Take 5 from 12, and how many remain?
37. Take 10 from 19, and how many remain?
38. Take 7 from 11, and how many remain?
39. Take 9 from 13, and how many remain?
40. Take 12 from 23, and how many remain?
41. What is the difference between 14 and 6?
42. What is the difference between 20 and 8?
43. What is the difference between 19 and 15?
44. What is the difference between 11 and 22?
45. What is the difference between 17 and 6?
46. What is the difference between 25 and 9?

---

9. *Subtraction* is the process of *finding* the difference between two numbers; the result is called the *Difference* or *Remainder.* The sign of subtraction is written thus, —, and is read *minus.* Placed between two numbers, or quantities, it shows that the one after it is to be taken from the one before it. 9 — 5 shows that 5 is to be subtracted from 9, and is read *nine minus five.*

1. How many are 10 — 6?
2. How many are 9 — 4?
3. How many are 12 — 7?
4. How many are 15 — 9?
5. How many are 20 — 8?
6. How many are 18 — 5?
7. How many are 17 — 3?
8. How many are 21 — 9?

9. How many are 16 — 7?
10. How many are 19 — 9?
11. How many are 21 — 12?
12. How many are 17 — 10?
13. How many are 18 — 9?
14. How many are 20 — 11?
15. How many are 25 — 10?
16. How many are 32 — 12?
17. How many are 46 — 10?
18. How many are 57 — 34?

ANALYSIS.   *57 is equal to 5 tens and 7 units, and 34 is equal to 3 tens and 4 units ; 3 tens from 5 tens leave 2 tens, or 20, and 4 units from 7 units leave 3 units, which added to 20 make 23.   Therefore, 57 — 34 = 23.*

19. 39 — 27 are how many?
20. 43 — 32 are how many?
21. 29 — 17 are how many?
22. 54 — 21 are how many?
23. 67 — 45 are how many?
24. 75 — 25 are how many?
25. 89 — 74 are how many?
26. 39 — 19 are how many?
27. 41 — 30 are how many?
28. 96 — 81 are how many?

---

10. 1. If you have 12 turkeys, and sell 9 of them, how many will you have left?

2. A grocer had 10 boxes of lemons, and sold 6 boxes; how many boxes had he left?

3. There are 20 men and 8 boys at work in a bookbindery; how many more men than boys are there?

4. From a cistern holding 36 barrels of water, 12 barrels leaked out; how many barrels remained?

5. A man, having 25 dollars due him, received a ton of hay worth 11 dollars, and the remainder in money ; how much money did he receive ?

6. There are 46 trees in an orchard ; 35 of them are apple trees and the remainder peach trees; how many are peach trees ?

7. From a piece of broadcloth containing 27 yards, 15 yards were cut ; how many yards remained ?

8. A jeweler bought a watch for 60 dollars, and sold it again for 75 dollars; how much did he gain ?

9. The whole number of pupils registered in a certain school is 87, and but 65 are in attendance ; how many are absent ?

10. Charles has 48 cents, and buys a slate for 16 cents ; how many cents has he left ?

11. There are 36 wild ducks in a flock, and a huntsman fires at them and kills 13 ; how many are left ?

12. A farmer sold a cow for 22 dollars that cost him 30 dollars; how much did he lose by the bargain ?

13. A grocer bought a quantity of sugar for 39 dollars, and sold it for 50 dollars ; how much did he gain ?

14. In a school are 27 boys and 35 girls; how many more girls than boys ?

15. The distance from Cincinnati to Miamisburg by railroad is 49 miles, and to Dayton 60 miles; what is the distance from Miamisburg to Dayton ?

16. In a warm day the thermometer indicated 85 degrees ; how many degrees was that above the freezing point, which is 32 degrees ?

17. A man died at the age of 77 years, having been married 49 years; what was his age when he married ?

11. 1. 4 and 7 and 9, less 8, are how many?
  2. 9 and 12 and 6, less 7, are how many?
  3. 14 and 10 and 12, less 24, are how many?
  4. 20 and 16 and 5, less 14, are how many?
  5. 44 and 20 and 10, less 50, are how many?
  6. 27 and 15 and 12, less 30, are how many?
  7. How many are 9 + 12 + 15 — 25?
  8. How many are 26 + 15 + 7 — 18?
  9. How many are 40 + 10 + 8 — 20?
  10. How much less than 64, is 25 + 20?
  11. How much less than 56, is 28 + 16?
  12. How much less than 100, is 46 + 34?
  13. How many are 16 + 12 + 9 + 5 — 32 + 8?
  14. How many are 33 + 28 + 9 — 30 + 15?
  15. How many are 84 + 26 + 15 — 70 + 25?
  16. A man, having 30 dollars, paid 15 dollars for a coat, 5 dollars for a vest, and 4 dollars for a hat; how much had he left?

ANALYSIS. *He had left the difference between 30 dollars and the sum of 15 + 5 + 4 dollars; 15 dollars and 5 dollars are 20 dollars, and 4 dollars are 24 dollars, and 30 dollars less 24 dollars are 6 dollars. Therefore, &c.*

  17. Ellen had 15 pinks, and she gave 6 to Mary and 4 to Jane; how many had she left?
  18. A woman, having 25 pounds of butter, sold 15 pounds at one time, and 10 pounds at another; how many pounds had she left?
  19. Amasa has 45 cents in three boxes; in the first are 15 cents, in the second 19 cents; how many cents are in the third box?
  20. A boy found 8 apples under one tree, 10 under another, and 6 under another; he ate 3, gave away 7, and carried the remainder home; how many did he take home?

21. Martin, having 27 marbles, gave 12 to Albert, and lost 5; how many had he left?

22. Reuben had 16 cents; Charles gave him 10, Elisha gave him 9, and Henry gave him enough to make his number 42; how many cents did Henry give him?

23. A merchant bought a hogshead of sugar for 50 dollars; he paid 6 dollars for freight and customs, and sold the whole for 75 dollars; how much did he gain?

24. A man bought a watch for 40 dollars, a chain for 15 dollars, and a key for 3 dollars, and he sold the whole for 50 dollars; how much did he lose by the bargain?

25. Sarah bought a comb for 12 cents, some ribbon for 16 cents, a thimble for 10 cents, and some thread for 6 cents; how much had she left of fifty cents, after paying for these articles?

26. A drover bought 9 sheep of one man, 12 of another, and 15 of another; he afterwards sold 8 and butchered 5; how many had he left?

27. From a piece of calico containing 26 yards Jane bought a dress of 9 yards, and Josephine another of 10 yards; how many yards were left in the piece?

28. Richard, receiving 45 dollars for labor, paid 20 dollars for a cow, 7 dollars for a barrel of flour, and 9 dollars for three cords of wood; how many dollars had he left?

29. Four men bought a horse for 80 dollars; the first gave 25 dollars, the second 20 dollars, and the third 18 dollars; how much did the fourth give?

30. A boy had 12 marbles; another boy gave him 10 more, another 9, and another enough more to make his number 40; how many did the last boy give him?

31. A man traveled 22 miles one day, and 26 miles the second day, and on the third day he traveled 30 miles on his return; how many miles was he from the place from which he first started?

32. George sold two dozen eggs for 20 cents, one bushel of apples for 37 cents, and received a pair of skates worth 75 cents; how much did he still owe for his skates?

33. A man owed his grocer 18 dollars, his tailor 20 dollars, and a merchant 25 dollars; he paid the grocer 10 dollars, the tailor 12 dollars, and the merchant 15 dollars; how much did he still owe them all?

34. Bought a horse for 90 dollars, a cutter for 40 dollars, and a harness for 20 dollars, and then sold the whole for 50 dollars more than the horse cost me; did I gain or lose by the bargain, and how much?

35. A lady bought a new bonnet for 7 dollars, a dress for 12 dollars, a pair of shoes for 2 dollars, and a parasol for 3 dollars; she gave the merchant 3 ten dollar bills; how many dollars must be returned?

36. A tailor bought a piece of cloth containing 31 yards, from which he sold 13 yards to one man, and 11 yards to another; how many yards were left of the piece?

37. A farmer had 45 sheep in one lot, 37 in another, and 30 in another; from the first he sold 20, from the second 15, and from the third 12; how many had he at first, and how many had he left?

38. A person, sitting down to play, counted his money, and found that he had 1 twenty dollar bill, 5 ten dollar bills, and 3 five dollar bills; when he got up from play, he had 7 ten dollar bills and 6 five dollar bills; did he gain or lose, and how much?

CHAPTER III.

MULTIPLICATION.

12.

2 times 1 are how many ? | 2 times 7 are how many ?
2 times 2 are how many ? | 2 times 8 are how many ?
2 times 3 are how many ? | 2 times 9 are how many ?
2 times 4 are how many ? | 2 times 10 are how many ?
2 times 5 are how many ? | 2 times 11 are how many ?
2 times 6 are how many ? | 2 times 12 are how many ?

3 times 1 are how many ? | 3 times 7 are how many ?
3 times 2 are how many ? | 3 times 8 are how many ?
3 times 3 are how many ? | 3 times 9 are how many ?
3 times 4 are how many ? | 3 times 10 are how many ?
3 times 5 are how many ? | 3 times 11 are how many ?
3 times 6 are how many ? | 3 times 12 are how many ?

4 times 1 are how many ? | 4 times 7 are how many ?
4 times 2 are how many ? | 4 times 8 are how many ?
4 times 3 are how many ? | 4 times 9 are how many ?
4 times 4 are how many ? | 4 times 10 are how many ?
4 times 5 are how many ? | 4 times 11 are how many ?
4 times 6 are how many ? | 4 times 12 are how many ?

1. How many are 2 times 6? 2 times 8? 2 times 7? 2 times 11? 2 times 9? 2 times 12?

2. How many are 3 times 5? 3 times 10? 3 times 9? 3 times 7? 3 times 6? 3 times 12?

3. How many are 4 times 4? 4 times 7? 4 times 9? 4 times 6? 4 times 10? 4 times 8?

4. At 9 dollars a ton, what will 3 tons of hay cost?

ANALYSIS. *Since one ton costs 9 dollars, 3 tons, which are 3 times 1 ton, will cost 3 times 9 dollars ; 3 times 9 dollars are 27 dollars. Therefore, at 9 dollars a ton, 3 tons of hay will cost 27 dollars.*

5. At 8 cents a quart, what will 4 quarts of blueberries cost ?

6. If you answer 11 questions at each recitation, how many questions would you answer at 3 recitations ? at 4 ?

7. What will 4 pairs of shoes cost at 12 shillings a pair ?

8. If a ream of paper cost 3 dollars, what will 2 reams cost ? 3 reams ? 4 reams ?

9. Eight New York shillings make a dollar ; how many shillings in 3 dollars ? in 4 dollars ? in 5 dollars ?

10. At 12 cents a yard, what will 3 yards of calico cost ? 4 yards ?

13.

5 times 1 are how many ?	5 times 7 are how many ?
5 times 2 are how many ?	5 times 8 are how many ?
5 times 3 are how many ?	5 times 9 are how many ?
5 times 4 are how many ?	5 times 10 are how many ?
5 times 5 are how many ?	5 times 11 are how many ?
5 times 6 are how many ?	5 times 12 are how many ?

6 times 1 are how many ?	6 times 7 are how many ?
6 times 2 are how many ?	6 times 8 are how many ?
6 times 3 are how many ?	6 times 9 are how many ?
6 times 4 are how many ?	6 times 10 are how many ?
6 times 5 are how many ?	6 times 11 are how many ?
6 times 6 are how many ?	6 times 12 are how many ?

7 times 1 are how many ?	7 times 7 are how many ?
7 times 2 are how many ?	7 times 8 are how many ?
7 times 3 are how many ?	7 times 9 are how many ?
7 times 4 are how many ?	7 times 10 are how many ?
7 times 5 are how many ?	7 times 11 are how many ?
7 times 6 are how many ?	7 times 12 are how many ?

1. How many are 5 times 6 ? 5 times 8 ? 5 times 4 ? 5 times 3 ? 5 times 7 ? 5 times 12 ? 5 times 9 ? 5 times 11?

2. How many are 6 times 3 ? 6 times 10 ? 6 times 6 ? 6 times 9 ? 6 times 7 ? 6 times 11 ? 6 times 8 ? 6 times 12 ?

3. How many are 7 times 2 ? 7 times 7 ? 7 times 4 ? 7 times 9 ? 7 times 12 ? 7 times 10 ? 7 times 8 ? 7 times 11 ? 7 times 6 ?

4. If you recite 8 perfect lessons in 1 week, how many would you recite in 5 weeks ? in 6 weeks ? in 7 weeks ?

5. What will 6 pounds of sugar cost at 10 cents a pound ? at 9 cents ?

6. If you write 5 lines a day, how many lines will you write in 4 days ? in 7 days ?

7. What cost 5 yards of ribbon, at 8 cents a yard ? at 9 cents ?

8. What cost 7 barrels of apples at 2 dollars a barrel ?

9. At 12 dollars a ton, what will 6 tons of hay cost ? 7 tons ? 5 tons ?

10. If a boat sail 9 miles an hour, how far will she sail in 4 hours ? in 6 hours ? in 7 hours ?

11. What cost 7 barrels of flour, at 11 dollars a barrel ?

12. There are 7 days in 1 week ; how many days in 5 weeks ? in 6 weeks ? in 9 weeks ?

14.

8 times 1 are how many ? 8 times 7 are how many ?
8 times 2 are how many ? 8 times 8 are how many ?
8 times 3 are how many ? 8 times 9 are how many ?
8 times 4 are how many ? 8 times 10 are how many ?
8 times 5 are how many ? 8 times 11 are how many ?
8 times 6 are how many ? 8 times 12 are how many ?

9 times 1 are how many ? | 9 times 7 are how many ?
9 times 2 are how many ? | 9 times 8 are how many ?
9 times 3 are how many ? | 9 times 9 are how many ?
9 times 4 are how many ? | 9 times 10 are how many ?
9 times 5 are how many ? | 9 times 11 are how many ?
9 times 6 are how many ? | 9 times 12 are how many ?

10 times 1 are how many ? | 10 times 7 are how many ?
10 times 2 are how many ? | 10 times 8 are how many ?
10 times 3 are how many ? | 10 times 9 are how many ?
10 times 4 are how many ? | 10 times 10 are how many ?
10 times 5 are how many ? | 10 times 11 are how many ?
10 times 6 are how many ? | 10 times 12 are how many ?

1. How many are 8 times 6 ? 8 times 4 ? 8 times 9 ? 8 times 5 ? 8 times 10 ? 8 times 7 ? 8 times 11 ? 8 times 8 ? 8 times 12 ?

2. How many are 9 times 3 ? 9 times 7 ? 9 times 4 ? 9 times 6 ? 9 times 8 ? 9 times 12 ? 9 times 9 ? 9 times 5 ? 9 times 11 ? 9 times 10 ?

3. How many are 10 times 10 ? 10 times 8 ? 10 times 4 ? 10 times 7 ? 10 times 11 ?

4. What will 8 barrels of flour cost, at 9 dollars a barrel ?

5. What will 9 chairs cost, at 10 shillings apiece ?

6. If 5 boys can sit on one bench, how many can sit on 7 benches ? on 8 benches ?

7. If Harvey can earn 10 dollars, in one month, how many dollars can he earn in 8 months ? in 9 months ? in 7 months ?

8. If 8 men can do a piece of work in 7 days, how many days will it take one man to do it ?

9. If two barrels of flour last 8 persons 3 months, how long will they last one person ?

10. How many dollars will buy 10 tons of hay, at 12 dollars a ton ?

11. A farmer divided his farm into 9 fields, containing 11 acres each; how many acres in his farm?

12. If a man travel 6 miles an hour, how far will he travel in 7 hours? in 8 hours? in 9 hours? in 6 hours?

13. When eggs are 11 cents a dozen, what will be the cost of 7 dozen? of 9 dozen? of 10 dozen?

15.

11 times 1 are how many?	11 times 7 are how many?
11 times 2 are how many?	11 times 8 are how many?
11 times 3 are how many?	11 times 9 are how many?
11 times 4 are how many?	11 times 10 are how many?
11 times 5 are how many?	11 times 11 are how many?
11 times 6 are how many?	11 times 12 are how many?

12 times 1 are how many?	12 times 7 are how many?
12 times 2 are how many?	12 times 8 are how many?
12 times 3 are how many?	12 times 9 are how many?
12 times 4 are how many?	12 times 10 are how many?
12 times 5 are how many?	12 times 11 are how many?
12 times 6 are how many?	12 times 12 are how many?

1. How many are 11 times 6? 11 times 10? 11 times 7? 11 times 12? 11 times 8? 11 times 11? 11 times 5?

2. How many are 12 times 10? 12 times 9? 12 times 7? 12 times 8? 12 times 6? 12 times 11? 12 times 5? 12 times 12?

3. What will be the cost of 11 bunches of grapes, at 10 cents a bunch?

4. What will be the cost of 12 barrels of pork, at 11 dollars a barrel?

5. What will 11 yards of cloth cost, at 6 dollars a yard?

6. In an orchard are 12 rows of trees, and 11 trees in each row ; how many trees in the orchard?

7. What will 11 turkeys cost at 6 dimes apiece? at 7 dimes?

8. At 12 dollars a hundred, what will 7 hundred oak posts cost? 9 hundred? 11 hundred?

9. At 9 dollars a week, what will 5 weeks' board cost? 8 weeks'? 11 weeks'? 12 weeks'?

10. If the fare for one person from Albany to Boston is 5 dollars, what will be the fare for 6 persons? for 9 persons? for 12 persons?

11. At 12 dollars a month, how many dollars can a man earn in 4 months? in 6 months? in 9 months? in 12 months?

12. If it take 9 yards of calico for one dress, how many yards will be required to make 4 dresses? 7 dresses?

13. If a farmer put his oats into 7 bins, each containing 12 bushels, how many bushels has he?

14. If I put 8 dollars in the savings bank every month, how many dollars will I deposit in 7 months? in 8 months? in 12 months?

15. What will 11 dozen of eggs cost, at 9 cents a dozen? at 10 cents? at 11 cents?

16. If a quantity of provision will last 9 men 12 days, how long will the same provision last one man?

17. When flour is 7 dollars a barrel, what must be paid for 7 barrels? for 8 barrels? for 9 barrels? for 11 barrels?

18. If 12 bushels of apples be picked from each of 11 trees, how many bushels will be picked from all?

16. *Multiplication* is the process of finding a number which shall contain one of two given numbers as many times as there are units in the other; the result is called the *Product.*

The sign of multiplication is written thus, ✕, and, placed between two numbers or quantities, shows that they are to be multiplied together. $5 \times 4 = 20$, shows that 5 *multiplied by* 4 is *equal to* 20. The sign is commonly called *times*. 5×4 is read 5 *times* 4.

1. 5×3 are how many ?
2. 7×4 are how many ?
3. 10×7 are how many ?
4. 3×8 are how many ?
5. 7×9 are how many ?
6. 12×6 are how many ?
7. 9×8 are how many ?
8. 8×11 are how many ?
9. 6×9 are how many ?
10. 5×7 are how many ?
11. 11×10 are how many ?
12. 8×4 are how many ?
13. 11×11 are how many ?
14. 12×12 are how many ?

15. What is the product of 7×6? of 9×5? of 7×7? of 11×6?

16. What is the product of $4 \times 3 \times 2$? of $5 \times 2 \times 3$? of $3 \times 3 \times 9$?

17. What will be the cost of 3 cows, at 23 dollars apiece ?

ANALYSIS. *Since* 1 *cow cost* 23 *dollars,* 3 *cows, which are* 3 *times* 1 *cow, will cost* 3 *times* 23 *dollars.* 23 *is equal to* 2 *tens and* 3 *units ;* 3 *times* 3 *units are* 9 *units, and* 3 *times* 2 *tens are* 6 *tens, or* 60 ; 60 *and* 9 *are* 69. *Therefore, if* 1 *cow cost* 23 *dollars,* 3 *cows will cost* 69 *dollars.*

18. At 31 cents a bushel, what will be the cost of 6 bushels of oats ?

19. What will be the cost of 7 bushels of apples, at 25 cents a bushel ?

20. If a man travel 26 miles in one day, how far can he travel in 10 days ?

21. Mary bought 6 yards of muslin at 18 cents a yard ; what was the cost of the whole ?

22. Ephraim is 17 years old, and his father is 4 times as old ; how old is his father ?

23. At 50 dollars a share, what will 7 shares of bank stock cost?

24. What will 9 pounds of tea cost, at 56 cents a pound?

25. At 44 cents a day, what will 10 days' labor amount to?

26. At 3 dollars a yard, what will be the cost of a piece of cloth containing 36 yards?

27. What will be the cost of 12 pounds of coffee, at 15 cents a pound?

28. If the cars run 24 miles an hour, how far will they run in 7 hours?

29. In an orchard are 16 peach trees, and 6 times as many apple trees; how many apple trees in the orchard?

30. What will be the cost of 45 lemons, at 5 cents apiece?

31. If 11 men can do a piece of work in 13 days, in what time will one man do the same work?

32. If a man labor 12 months for 17 dollars a month, how much will his wages amount to?

33. At 3 dollars a barrel, what will be the cost of 28 barrels of potatoes?

34. If in an orchard are 12 rows of trees, and 32 trees in each row, how many trees in the orchard?

35. If a man can dig 28 bushels of potatoes in one day, how many bushels can he dig in 3 days? in 4 days? in 5 days?

36. At 80 dollars apiece, what will be the cost of 3 horses? of 4 horses? of 6 horses?

37. At 43 dollars an acre, what will 10 acres of land cost? 12 acres?

38. If 8 horses eat 3 bushels of oats in one day, how many bushels will they eat in 7 days? in 9 days?

17. 1. What will be the cost of 6 tons of coal, at 5 dollars a ton, and of 4 cords of wood at 3 dollars a cord ?

ANALYSIS. *They will cost the sum of the products of 6 × 5 dollars, and of 4 × 3 dollars; 6 times 5 dollars are 30 dollars, and 4 times 3 dollars are 12 dollars; 30 dollars and 12 dollars are 42 dollars. Therefore, &c.*

2. A farmer sold 12 sheep at 4 dollars a head, and 9 lambs at 2 dollars each; how many dollars did he receive for all ?

3. What will be the cost of 5 pounds of coffee at 15 cents a pound, and 14 pounds of rice at 6 cents a pound ?

4. If two persons start from the same point, and travel in opposite directions, one at the rate of 6 miles an hour, and the other 4 miles an hour, how far apart will they be in 7 hours ? in 9 hours ? in 12 hours ?

5. If they travel in the same direction, how far apart will they be in 5 hours ? in 7 hours ? in 24 hours ?

6. If I hire a man and his son to labor, the father at 14 shillings a day, and the son at 8 shillings, how much will be due them both in 6 days ? in 9 days ?

7. Asa has 16 marbles, and Omar 3 times as many ; how many have both ?

8. A drover bought 28 sheep at 3 dollars a head, and 5 cows at 26 dollars apiece; what was the cost of the whole ?

9. Justin bought 9 oranges at 4 cents apiece, 7 lemons at 3 cents apiece, and 10 lead pencils at 2 cents apiece; how much was the cost of the whole ?

10. Charles is twice as old as Byron, and Byron is 14 years old ; what is the sum of their ages ?

11. In a school-room 16 pupils can sit on each

of 5 seats, 8 on each of 3 seats, and 20 on the remainder of the seats; how many pupils can be seat-
ed in the room?

12. A farmer has 30 sheep in each of 3 pastures,
35 in each of 2 pastures, and 40 in another pasture; how many sheep has he in all?

13. If one boy earns 12 cents a day, another 15
cents a day, and another 20 cents a day, how much
can the 3 boys earn in 5 days?

14. A man bought 9 yards of cloth for a suit of
clothes, at 5 dollars a yard; he paid 7 dollars for
making the coat, 2 dollars for making the pantaloons,
and 1 dollar for making the vest; what did his suit
cost him?

---

18. 1. A farmer bought a horse for 85 dollars,
for which he gave 7 tons of hay at 9 dollars a ton,
and the remainder in money; how much money did
he pay?

ANALYSIS. *He paid in money, the difference between
85 dollars and the product of 7 times 9 dollars; 7 times 9
dollars are 63 dollars, and 85 dollars less 63 dollars are 22
dollars. Therefore, &c.*

2. John worked 5 days for 15 cents a day, and
Norman worked 4 days for 20 cents a day; how
much more did Norman earn than John?

3. A drover bought 35 sheep at 2 dollars a head,
and sold them for 90 dollars; how much did he gain?

4. A mechanic earned 32 dollars a month for
five months, and his apprentice 12 dollars a month
for the same time; how much more did the one earn
than the other?

5. If a man earn 90 cents a day, and pay 40 cents
a day for his board, how much will he save in 6 days?

3

6. A farmer sold a grocer 7 pounds of butter at 20 cents a pound, and received in payment 12 pounds of fish at 6 cents a pound; how much was still due the farmer?

7. How much difference does Mr. Jones receive, by exchanging 5 cows at 18 dollars a head, for 7 head of young cattle, at 9 dollars each?

8. A merchant poured into a cask 14 quarts of camphene 3 different times, and from the same cask filled 2 cans, holding 8 quarts each, and 3 jugs, holding 6 quarts each; how many quarts remained in the cask?

9. Nellie picked 6 quarts of blackberries, and Laura picked 4 times as many, wanting 5 quarts; how many quarts did Laura pick?

10. What is the difference in the cost of 30 yards of cloth at 4 dimes a yard, and 25 yards at 3 dimes a yard?

11. A lady bought 6 yards of satin, at 2 dollars a yard, 2 shawls at 9 dollars each, and some lace for 3 dollars; she paid 4 ten dollar bills; how much ought she to receive back?

12. A drover bought 50 sheep for 125 dollars; he sold 30 at 4 dollars a head, and the remainder at 3 dollars a head; how many dollars did he gain by the bargain?

13. Three boys talking of their money, one said he had 35 cents, another said he had twice as many, and the third said he had as many as both the others, wanting 10 cents; how many cents had the last?

14. Two men bought a horse for 75 dollars; they paid 2 dollars a week for keeping him, and at the end of 12 weeks sold him for 90 dollars; how much did they lose by their bargain?

15. A man, owing 100 dollars, gave a sleigh worth 40 dollars, 12 cords of wood, at 3 dollars a cord,

and the remainder in money ; how much money did he pay ?

16. I bought a book-case for 28 dollars, a table for 14 dollars, and 6 chairs at 2 dollars each ; I paid for the table ; how much did I still owe ?

17. If a blacksmith earn 14 shillings a day, and a joiner 11 shillings a day, what will the difference in their earnings amount to in 12 days ?

18. Perry paid 3 cents for a lemon, Elisha twice as much for a pineapple, and for a melon Albert paid 5 times as much, lacking 15 cents, as was paid for both the lemon and the pineapple ; what would be the cost of 3 melons at the same rate ?

19. At a public meeting are 35 gentlemen, and 3 times as many ladies lacking 30 ; how many ladies are there, and how many ladies and gentlemen ?

20. Peter has 4 times 5 peaches, and Marcus has 3 times 6 ; how many will they both have left after Peter gives away 7, and Marcus 5 ?

21. How many are 4 times 20, plus 3 times 10 ?

22. How many are 7 times 15, plus 9 times 12 ?

23. How many are 12 times 11, minus 10 times 7 ?

24. How many are 10 times 11, less 15, plus 6 times 5 ?

25. How much less is 7 times 14, than 3 times 40 ?

26. How much less is 10 times 10, than 6 times 20 plus 25 ?

27. How much more is 8 times 16, than 7 times 13 minus 11 ?

28. How many are 9 times 12, plus $22 + 10 - 30$?

29. How many are $15 \times 12, + 20 \times 5$?

30. How many are $40 \times 4, + 27 \times 3$?

31. How many are $16 \times 9, - 13 \times 6$?

32. How many are $10 + 12, \times 6, - 40$?

33. How many are $14 \times 8, + 18, + 12, - 7$?

CHAPTER IV.

DIVISION.

19. 1. WHEN wheat is 2 dollars a bushel, how many bushels can be bought for 12 dollars ?

ANALYSIS. *Since 2 dollars will buy 1 bushel, 12 dollars will buy as many bushels as 2 dollars, the price of 1 bushel, is contained times in 12 dollars ; 2 dollars is contained in 12 dollars 6 times. Therefore, at 2 dollars a bushel, 6 bushels of wheat can be bought for 12 dollars.*

2. How many peaches at 2 cents apiece, can be bought for 18 cents ?

3. If you can buy one lead pencil for 3 cents, how many can you buy for 24 cents ?

4. For 16 dollars, how many cords of wood can be bought at 4 dollars a cord ?

5. At 3 cents apiece, how many oranges can be bought for 21 cents ?

6. In how many days can a man earn 20 dollars, if he earn 2 dollars a day ?

7. Edward has 15 peaches, which he wishes to divide equally among his 3 brothers ; how many must he give to each ?

8. How many times 2 in 8 ? in 6 ? in 10 ? in 14 ? in 16 ? in 20 ? in 24 ?

9. How many times 3 in 6 ? in 12 ? in 18 ? in 21 ? in 9 ? in 27 ? in 33 ? in 24 ? in 36 ?

10. How many times 4 in 12 ? in 8 ? in 16 ? in 20 ? in 36 ? in 24 ? in 40 ? in 32 ? in 48 ?

11. How many tons of coal, at 4 dollars a ton, can be bought for 48 dollars ?

12. If one penholder can be bought for 4 cents, how many can be bought for 20 cents ? for 32 cents ? for 40 cents ?

13. Paid 36 dollars for 3 gold chains; what was the cost of each ?

14. How many barrels of apples, at 3 dollars a barrel, can be bought for 36 dollars ?

15. If you give 44 cents to 4 beggars, how many do you give to each ?

16. If a man walk 3 miles an hour, how many hours will it take him to walk 30 miles ?

17. Bought 4 barrels of flour for 28 dollars ; what was the cost of one barrel ?

18. If I pay 27 cents for 3 pounds of sugar, how much do I pay a pound ?

19. 15 are how many times 3 ? 5 ?

20. 36 are how many times 3 ? 6 ? 4 ?

21. 42 are how many times 6 ? 7 ? 3 ?

22. 24 are how many times 2 ? 6 ? 4 ? 8 ?

23. 16 are how many times 4 ? 2 ? 8 ?

24. 40 are how many times 8 ? 5 ? 4 ?

25. 72 are how many times 8 ? 6 ? 12 ?

26. 56 are how many times 7 ? 8 ? 4 ?

27. 48 are how many times 4 ? 6 ? 8 ? 12 ?

28. 32 are how many times 8 ? 2 ? 4 ?

29. 30 are how many times 5 ? 6 ? 3 ?

---

20. 1. How many spools of thread, at 5 cents a spool, can be bought for 40 cents ? for 50 cents ?

2. When lard is 7 cents a pound, how many pounds can be bought for 56 cents ? for 63 cents ?

3. If a farmer divide 84 bushels of potatoes equally among 7 laborers, how many bushels will each receive ?

4. If an orchard contain 64 trees, and 8 trees in a row, how many rows are there ?

5. If a man travel 72 miles in 6 hours, how far does he travel in one hour ?

6. Levi paid 7 cents for his ball; how many balls at the same price could he buy for 28 cents? for 56 cents? for 63 cents? for 84 cents?

7. How many bins will be required to hold 72 bushels of wheat, if each bin contain 8 bushels?

8. At 5 dollars a week, how long will it take a man to earn 45 dollars? 50 dollars?

9. At 8 cents a pound, how many pounds of sugar can be bought for 96 cents?

10. If a man spend 6 cents a day for cigars, how many days will 60 cents last him?

11. A man bought some sheep for 48 dollars, at 4 dollars apiece; how many sheep did he buy?

12. If one man can do a job of work in 60 days, in what time can 5 men do the same work?

13. 45 are how many times 5? 9? 3?

14. 36 are how many times 4? 6? 9? 12?

15. 80 are how many times 10? 8? 4? 5?

16. 96 are how many times 8? 6? 12? 4?

17. 44 are how many times 11? 4? 2?

18. 24 are how many times 2? 8? 4? 6? 12?

19. 60 are how many times 6? 5? 10? 12?

20. 63 are how many times 9? 3? 7?

21. 84 are how many times 7? 12? 4? 6?

22. 90 are how many times 9? 6? 10?

23. 108 are how many times 12? 9? 6?

24. 100 are how many times 10? 20? 5?

25. 99 are how many times 9? 11? 3?

26. 81 are how many times 9?

27. 66 are how many times 11? 6? 3?

28. 75 are how many times 15? 5? 25?

29. 88 are how many times 4? 11? 8?

30. 120 are how many times 12? 10? 8?

31. 140 are how many times 7? 10? 20?

32. 200 are how many times 20? 40? 50?

21. 1. If 6 men receive 72 dollars for building a barn, how many dollars will each man receive?

NOTE. If the pupil is sufficiently acquainted with *Fractions,* the following *Analysis* is often preferred. *

ANALYSIS. *If 6 men receive 72 dollars, 1 man, which is ⅙ of 6 men, will receive ⅙ of 72 dollars ; ⅙ of 72 dollars is 12 dollars. Therefore if 6 men receive 72 dollars for building a barn, each man will receive 12 dollars.*

2. If 81 cents be paid for 9 dozen of eggs, what will be the cost of 1 dozen?

3. A mechanic sold a wagon for 77 dollars, and took his pay in hay, at 11 dollars a ton; how many tons did he receive?

4. How long will it take 12 men to perform a piece of work that 1 man can do in 48 days?

5. Paid 108 dollars for 9 thousand feet of lumber; what was the cost of a thousand feet?

6. How many barrels of flour can be bought for 56 dollars, at 7 dollars a barrel? at 8 dollars?

7. How many cows, at 12 dollars a head, can be bought for 60 dollars? for 96 dollars? for 120 dollars?

8. When steak is 10 cents a pound, how many pounds can be bought for 50 cents? for 80 cents? for 100 cents?

9. At 11 cents a pound, how many pounds of sugar can be bought for 88 cents? for 99 cents?

* When it is necessary to express a quantity less than a unit, we may regard the unit as divided into some number of equal parts, and use one of these parts as a new unit of less value than the unit divided. Thus, if a yard be divided into *two* equal parts, each of the parts is called *one half;* when into *three* equal parts, each of the parts is called *one third;* when into *four* equal parts, each of the parts is called *one fourth;* when into *five* equal parts, each of the parts is called *one-fifth;* *two* of the parts, *two fifths,* &c.; when into *six* equal parts, each of the parts is called *one sixth; two* of the parts, *two sixths, three* of the parts, *three sixths,* &c.

10. A man planted an orchard of 132 trees, and put 11 trees in a row; how many rows in the orchard?

11. A farmer sold a horse for 120 dollars; how many cows at 12 dollars each would pay for the horse? How many young cattle at 8 dollars each? How many sheep at 5 dollars each?

12. If 25 sheep cost 75 dollars, what will 1 sheep cost?

13. If a boy read 7 pages a day, how long will it take him to read 56 pages? to read 84 pages? 98 pages?

14. At 15 cents a pound, how many pounds of coffee can be bought for 45 cents? for 60 cents? for 90 cents?

15. If 1 man can do a piece of work in 72 days, in what time can 6 men do it? 8 men? 9 men? 12 men?

16. If a certain quantity of provision will last 1 man 36 days, how many days will it last 4 men? 9 men? 12 men?

17. A man earns 66 dollars in 11 weeks; how much does he earn in 1 week? how much in 1 day?

18. If a painter receive 100 dollars for painting 5 carriages, how much does he receive apiece?

19. How many lots containing 12 acres each can be sold from a farm of 120 acres? how many lots of 20 acres each?

20. If a steamboat run 11 miles an hour, how long will she be in running 44 miles? 88 miles? 110 miles?

21. How many men, at 8 dollars a month, can be hired one month for 96 dollars? how many at 12 dollars? how many at 16 dollars?

22. If I travel 120 miles in 6 days, how many miles do I travel in 1 day?

22.   1. If 3 pounds of coffee cost 27 cents, what will 6 pounds cost?

ANALYSIS. *If 3 pounds of coffee cost 27 cents, 1 pound, which is 1 third of 3 pounds, will cost 1 third of 27 cents, or 9 cents. If 1 pound cost 9 cents, 6 pounds, which are 6 times 1 pound, will cost 6 times 9 cents, or 54 cents. Therefore, if 3 pounds of coffee cost 27 cents, 6 pounds will cost 54 cents.*

Or thus : *6 pounds will cost 6 times 1 third of 27 cents; 1 third of 27 cents is 9 cents, and 6 times 9 cents are 54 cents. Therefore, &c.*

Or 6 pounds, which are 2 times 3 pounds, will cost 2 times 27 cents, &c.

2. If 4 yards of broadcloth cost 20 dollars, what will 9 yards cost?

3. If 6 barrels of flour cost 54 dollars, what will 7 barrels cost?

4. If 9 yards of ribbon cost 72 cents, what will 4 yards cost?

5. If a man travel 40 miles in 8 hours, how far will he travel in 6 hours? in 9 hours?

6. If 5 coats can be cut from 20 yards of cloth, how many yards would be required to cut 7 coats?

7. If 9 weeks' board cost 45 dollars, what will 4 weeks' board cost? 7 weeks'? 12 weeks'?

8. If a boy earn 60 cents in 5 days, how many cents will he earn in 12 days? in 20 days?

9. What will be the cost of 10 cords of wood, if 6 cords cost 24 dollars?

10. What will be the cost of 14 dozen of eggs, if 12 dozen cost 120 cents?

11. If 18 apples are worth 6 peaches, how many apples are 15 peaches worth? 20 peaches?

12. If a stage coach run 48 miles in 8 hours, in how many hours will it run 60 miles?

13. If 15 yards of cloth cost 75 dollars, what will 40 yards cost?

4 *

14. How many melons can be bought for 100 cents, at the rate of 3 for 60 cents?

15. What will 42 pounds of beef cost, if 7 pounds cost 56 cents?

16. When apples are sold at the rate of 4 barrels for 8 dollars, how many barrels must be given for 3 tons of coal at 6 dollars a ton?

17. How many dozen of eggs, at 12 cents a dozen, will pay for 15 pounds of sugar, at 8 cents a pound?

18. How many gallons of molasses, at 36 cents a gallon, will pay for 20 pounds of lard, worth 10 cents a pound?

19. If a farmer sell 5 firkins of butter, worth 12 dollars a firkin, for cloth worth 4 dollars a yard, how many yards will he receive?

20. If 5 barrels of cider are worth 15 dollars, how many hundred weight of pork, worth 6 dollars a hundred weight, would 8 barrels of cider buy?

21. If 6 bushels of wheat are worth 12 dollars, how many bushels of wheat must be given for 9 tons of hay, worth 10 dollars a ton?

22. At the rate of 3 for 4 cents, how many pears can be bought for 24 cents?

ANALYSIS. *Since 4 cents will buy 3 pears, 24 cents will buy as many times 3 pears as 4 cents is contained times in 24 cents ; 4 cents are contained in 24 cents 6 times, and 6 times 3 are 18 pears. Therefore, if 3 pears can be bought for 4 cents, 18 pears may be bought for 24 cents.*

23. A man paid 72 cents for some oranges, at the rate of 5 for 12 cents; how many oranges did he buy?

24. How many pounds of nails may be bought for 60 cents, at the rate of 4 pounds for 20 cents?

25. When eggs are sold at the rate of 9 for 11 cents, how many must be sold to receive 99 cents?

26. At the rate of 16 miles in 4 hours, how many miles would a man travel in 12 hours?

27. If 3 men can do a piece of work in 12 days, how many days will it take 9 men to do the same?

ANALYSIS. *If 3 men can do the work in* 12 *days,* 9 *men can do it in* $\frac{1}{9}$ *of* 3 *times* 12 *days ;* 3 *times* 12 *days are* 36 *days, and* $\frac{1}{9}$ *of* 36 *days are* 4 *days. Therefore, &c.*

28. If 6 men can build a wall in 8 days, how many men will be required to build it in 3 days?

29. If 4 men can dig a ditch in 10 days, how many days will it take 1 man to dig it? 5 men? 8 men?

30. How long will it take 7 men to reap a field, if it take 14 men 2 days to reap it?

31. If 5 men can build a barn in 8 days, how many men would be required to build it in 1 day? in 2 days? in 4 days?

32. A man bought some oranges for 44 cents, at the rate of 5 for 11 cents, and divided them equally among his 4 children; how many did he give to each?

33. If 15 days' work will pay for 10 cords of wood, at 3 dollars a cord, what is the price of 1 day's labor?

34. A man engaged to labor 5 months for 80 dollars, but by request continued 3 months longer, at the same rate; what amount will be due him for the whole time?

35. If you pay 60 cents for some lemons, at the rate of 6 for 10 cents, and sell them at the rate of 9 for 20 cents, how many cents will you gain by the operation?

36. If two ships are 120 miles apart, and sail directly toward each other, one at the rate of 9 miles an hour, and the other at the rate of 11 miles an hour, how many hours before they will meet?

23. *Division* is the process of finding how many times one number is contained in another; and the result is called the *Quotient.* The sign of division is written thus, $\div$, and, placed between two numbers or quantities, shows that the one on the left is to be divided by the one on the right. $24 \div 8 = 3$ shows that 24 *divided* by 8 is *equal to* 3.

1. How many times 9 are 6 times 6 ?
2. How many times 4 are 5 times 8 ?
3. How many times 8 are 6 times 12 ?
4. How many times 10 are 5 times 20 ?
5. How many times 15 are 3 times 25 ?
6. How many times 20 are 10 times 12 ?
7. How many times 16 are 8 times 8 ?
8. How many times 28 are 7 times 16 ?
9. How many times 25 are 5 times 30 ?
10. How many times 20 are 12 times 10 ?
11. 16 times 4 are how many times 8 ?
12. 9 times 12 are how many times 6 ?
13. 8 times 14 are how many times 16 ?
14. 4 times 42 are how many times 12 ?
15. 7 times 18 are how many times 9 ?
16. 14 times 10 are how many times 28 ?
17. 12 times 8 + 4 are how many times 10 ?
18. 6 times 15 + 20 are how many times 12 ? *
19. How many times 9 + 3 are 7 times 13 less 10 ?
20. How many times 18 — 4 are 8 times 12 + 2 ?
21. In 8 × 12, how many times 64 ÷ 8 ?
22. In 6 × 20 + 12, how many times 55 ÷ 5 ?
23. In 48 + 24 divided by 6, how many times 4 ?
24. How many times 12 — 7 are 9 times 8 ?
25. How many times 9 + 6 in 6 times 12 + 3 ?
26. How many times 27 ÷ 9 + 7 × 3 are 8 × 11 + 20 ?

---

* Each sign affects *only* the number placed after it. When there is a remainder in the result, let it simply be mentioned as such.

24. 1. How many vests, at 5 dollars each, will pay for 7 weeks' board, at 6 dollars a week, and 18 dollars borrowed money?

2. If a man receive 16 pounds of sugar in exchange for 20 pounds of cheese at 8 cents a pound, what is the price of the sugar per pound?

3. James paid 36 cents for some oranges at 3 cents apiece, and, after eating 5 of them, he gave the remainder, at 4 cents apiece, for a knife; how much did the knife cost him?

4. Omar bought 30 peaches at the rate of 2 for 3 cents, and, after eating 3 of them and giving 3 to his brother, he sold the remainder at the rate of 3 for 7 cents; did he gain or lose by the bargain, and how much?

5. A farmer sold 9 sheep at 12 shillings a head, and 11 bushels of oats at 2 shillings a bushel; how many yards of cloth, at 10 shillings a yard, will pay the debt?

6. If I buy 40 turkeys at the rate of 5 for 3 dollars, and sell them at the rate of 8 for 7 dollars, how much will I gain by the operation?

7. If a drover buy 24 lambs for 30 dollars, at how much must he sell them a head to gain 18 dollars on the cost?

8. If 5 men buy a mowing machine for 120 dollars, and rent it 3 weeks for 15 dollars a week, and then sell it for 100 dollars, what is each man's share of the gain?

9. If 5 barrels of flour are worth 30 dollars, how many yards of cloth worth 3 dollars a yard will 2 barrels of the flour buy?

10. Four men agree to build 120 rods or wall for 48 dollars, and to share equally; but when the wall is half built, 2 men quit, and the others finish it; how many dollars must each receive?

11. How many sheep can I buy for 75 dollars at the rate of 3 for 7 dollars, and have 12 dollars left?

12. A man, having 80 dollars, bought 9 cords of wood at 4 dollars a cord, 3 barrels of flour at 8 dollars a barrel, and the remainder he expended for cloth at 4 dollars a yard; how many yards of cloth did he buy?

13. If 4 bushels of wheat are worth 12 bushels of corn, how many bushels of corn are equal in value to 10 bushels of wheat?

14. If 12 bushels of wheat make 3 barrels of flour, how many bushels of wheat will make 7 barrels?

15. A cistern holding 140 gallons has a pipe by which 30 gallons will run into the cistern in one hour, and another that will discharge 20 gallons in an hour; when both are running, in what time will the cistern be filled?

16. If a quantity of provision serve 7 men 12 days, how long would it serve 4 men?

17. A merchant bought 15 bushels of clover seed for 75 dollars; he wishes to keep 3 bushels for his own use, and to sell the remainder so as to make 9 dollars on the first cost of the whole; how much must he ask a bushel?

18. A man bought a span of horses for 80 dollars each; he spent 40 dollars in fitting them for market, and then sold them for 300 dollars; what was his gain on each horse?

19. A tailor bought 15 yards of one kind of cloth for 60 dollars, and 25 yards of another kind for 75 dollars; what was the difference in the price per yard?

20. A thief, having 36 miles the start of an officer, travels at the rate of 6 miles an hour; the officer pursues at the rate of 9 miles an hour; in how many hours will he overtake the thief?

21. Add 5 to 22, divide the sum by 9, multiply the quotient by 12, subtract 6 from the product, and add 10 to the remainder ; what will be the result?

22. Divide 40 by 8, multiply the quotient by 9, to the product add 11, from the sum take 6, and what will remain?

23. Multiply 20 by 4, subtract 40, add 10, divide by 5, multiply by 7, and what is the result?

24. From 36 subtract 6, divide the remainder by 5, multiply the quotient by 12, add 15 to the product, subtract 77 from the sum, divide the remainder by 10, and what will be the quotient?

25. Add 5 and 7 to 8, multiply the sum by 3, from the product subtract 5, divide the remainder by 11, multiply the quotient by 6, add 20 to the product, and what will be the sum?

26. Subtract 10 from 6 multiplied by 8, to the remainder add 4, divide the sum by 6, multiply the quotient by 11, subtract 7 from the product, divide the remainder by 10, add 30 to the quotient, and what will be the sum?

27. Multiply 15 by 5, add 5, divide by 8, multiply by 6, subtract 10, divide by 5, add 2, multiply by 11, and what will be the product?

28. $10 + 8 \div 6 \times 9 - 7 \times 5 + 20 \div 10 + 8 =$ how many?

29. $8 \times 9 \div 12 + 3 \times 5 + 10 \div 11 \times 8 + 20 \div 12 + 4 \times 7 - 3 =$ how many?

30. $25 - 5 \div 2 \times 9 + 10 \div 20 \times 12 + 15 - 5 \div 7 + 8 + 2 =$ how many?

31. $36 \div 9 \times 12 + 8 \div 7 \times 5 + 10 - 25 \div 5 + 4 \times 9 - 11 \div 10 \times 6 \div 3 =$ how many?

NOTE. The above examples will afford a thorough and profitable mental drill to the pupil, and also familiarize the signs and terms used in the preceding pages, and which must be well understood in the commencement of the study of Written Arithmetic. The teacher can extend the number of examples at pleasure.

CHAPTER V.

REDUCTION.

25. TABLE OF UNITED STATES MONEY.

10 mills (m.)	make	1 cent,	c.
10 cents	"	1 dime,	d.
10 dimes	"	1 dollar,	$.
10 dollars	"	1 eagle,	E.

NOTE. Dollars and cents are separated by a period (.); thus, $2.10, is read 2 dollars 10 cents.

A *Simple Number* contains but one name or denomination; thus, 5, 84, 12 bushels, 65 dollars, are simple numbers.

A *Compound Number* contains two or more names or denominations; thus, 5 dollars 25 cents, 16 bushels 3 pecks, 3 days 10 hours, are compound numbers.

Reduction is the process of changing numbers from one denomination to another, without altering their value; thus, changing pounds to ounces, ounces to pounds, dollars to cents, &c., is reduction.

1. How many mills in 2 cents? in 3 cents?
2. How many cents in 1 dime? in 3 dimes?
3. How many dimes in 3 dollars? in 4 dollars?
4. How many dollars in 2 eagles? in 5 eagles?
5. How many cents in 4 dimes and 7 cents?
6. How many dimes in 3 dollars and 6 dimes?
7. If James earned 12 dollars, and his father 3 eagles, how many dollars did they both earn?
8. A man has 4 eagles, 4 five dollar bills, and 4 dimes; how many dollars and cents has he?
9. How many dimes are equal to 40 cents? to 70 cents?
10. What is the difference in the cost of 8 yards of cloth at 2 dimes a yard, and 6 yards at 30 cents a yard?

26.   TABLE OF ENGLISH MONEY.

·4 farthings (far.)	make	1 penny,	d.
12 pence	"	1 shilling,	s.
20 shillings	"	1 pound,	£.

NOTE. A sovereign (sov.) is equal in value to one pound.

1. How many farthings in 1 penny? in 3 pence? in 6 pence? in 9 pence?

2. How many pence in 1 shilling? in 4 shillings? in 5 shillings? in 9 shillings? in 10 shillings?

3. How many pence in 8 farthings? in 24 farthings? in 48 farthings?

4. How many shillings in 24 pence? in 84 pence? in 108 pence?

5. How many pounds in 40 shillings? in 120 shillings?

6. At 5 shillings a yard, how many pounds will 20 yards of carpeting cost?

7. At 7 shillings a pair, how many pairs of shoes can be bought for 2 sovereigns?

---

27.   TABLE OF TROY WEIGHT.

24 grains (gr.)	make	1 pennyweight,	pwt.
20 pennyweights	"	1 ounce,	oz.
12 ounces	"	1 pound,	lb.

1. How many grains in 2 pennyweights? in 4?

2. How many pennyweights in 3 ounces? in 5?

3. How many pennyweights in 96 grains? in 124 grains?

4. In 120 pennyweights how many ounces? in 200 pennyweights?

5. What will a gold chain, weighing 15 pennyweights cost, at 8 dimes a pennyweight? how many dollars and cents?

4

28.   TABLE OF AVOIRDUPOIS WEIGHT

16 drams (dr.)   make   1 ounce,   oz.
16 ounces   "   1 pound,   lb.
100 pounds   "   1 hundred weight, cwt.
20 hundred weight   "   1 ton.   T.

1. How many drams in 3 ounces? in 4 ounces? in 6 ounces?

2. How many ounces in 32 drams? in 48 drams? in 64 drams?

3. How many ounces in 3 pounds? in 5 lbs.? in 7 lbs.?

4. How many ounces in 2 lbs. 6 oz.? in 4 lbs. 10 oz.?

5. In 3 cwt. and 5 lbs., how many pounds?

6. In 5 pounds, how many ounces?

7. How many pounds in 3 cwt.? in 6 cwt.? in 9 cwt.?

8. In 16 tons, how many cwt.? in 25 tons?

9. In 1 ton and 5 cwt., how many cwt.? how many pounds?

10. How many dollars will 3 cwt. of flour cost, if 25 pounds cost 5 dimes?

11. What will 1 ton and 5 cwt. of hay cost, if 5 cwt. cost 3 dollars?

12. What will 2 cwt. 10 lbs. of beef cost at 6 cents a pound?

13. If 8 ounces of tea cost 4 dimes, what will 2 pounds cost?

14. What will be the cost of 4 cwt. of sugar, at 7 cents a pound?

15. Which will cost the more, 5 cwt. of fish at 6 cents a pound, or 3 tons of hay at 50 cents a cwt.?

16. What will 1 ton of hay cost at 1 cent a pound?

29.   TABLE OF LONG MEASURE.

12	inches (in.)	make 1 foot,	ft.
3	feet	" 1 yard,	yd.
5½	yards, or 16½ feet,	" 1 rod,	rd.
40	rods	" 1 furlong,	fur.
8	furlongs, or 320 rods,	" 1 mile,	mi.
3	miles	" 1 league,	lea.
69½	miles	" 1 degree,	deg. or °.
360	degrees	" 1 circle of the earth.	

1. How many inches in 3 ft.? in 5 ft.? in 10 ft.? in 12 ft.?

2. How many feet in 4 yards? in 6 yards? in 9 yards?

3. How many yards in 15 feet? in 24 feet?

4. How many yards in 2 rods? in 4 rods?

5. How many furlongs in 5 miles? in 7 miles and 4 furlongs?

6. How many furlongs in 80 rods? in 120 rods? in 160 rods?

7. In 2 miles 4 fur. 20 rods, how many rods?

8. How many leagues in 9 miles? in 18 miles? in 36 miles?

9. How many inches in 3 yds. 1 ft. 10 in.?

10. In 108 inches how many yards? in 144 inches?

11. If a man travel 5 miles an hour, how long will it take him to travel 20 leagues?

12. If a ship sail 20 leagues a day, how long will it take her to sail from New York to Liverpool, it being 3000 miles?

13. In 100 inches how many yards, feet, and inches?

14. At 8 dimes a foot, how many dollars will 3 yds. 1 ft. of iron railing cost?

15. In 2 rods 5 feet, how many inches?

30. TABLE OF CLOTH MEASURE.

$2\frac{1}{4}$ inches (in.)   make   1 nail,   na.
4 nails   "   1 quarter of a yard, qr.
4 quarters   "   1 yard,   yd.

1. How many nails in 3 qrs.? in 5 qrs.?
2. How many nails in 2 yds. 2 qrs.?
3. How many quarters in 5 yds.? in 6 yds. 3 qrs.?
4. How many yards in 16 qrs.? in 56 qrs.?
5. How many qrs. in 36 nails? in 64 na.?
6. How many qrs. in 5 yds.? in 6 yds.? in 7 yds.?
7. In 4 yards, how many nails?
8. In 6 yards, how many qrs.?
9. In 123 nails, how many yards?

---

31. TABLE OF LAND OR SQUARE MEASURE.

144 square inches (sq. in.) make 1 square foot, sq. ft.
  9 square feet   "   1 square yard, sq. yd.
$30\frac{1}{4}$ square yards   "   1 square rod, P.
 40 square rods   "   1 rood,   R.
  4 roods   "   1 acre,   A.
640 acres   "   1 square mile, Sq. M.

1. How many square feet in 5 square yards? in 10 square yards? in 20 square yards?
2. How many square yards in 36 sq. ft.? in 72 sq. ft.? in 108 sq. ft.?
3. How many square rods in 3 roods? in 5 roods? in 7 roods?
4. How many acres in 20 roods? in 80 roods?
5. At 4 dollars a square rod, what would 2 roods 10 rods of land cost?

32. TABLE OF CUBIC MEASURE.

1728 cubic inches (cu. in.) make 1 cubic foot, cu. ft.
27 " feet " 1 cubic yard, cu. yd.
24¾ " feet " 1 perch of stone, Pch.
16 " feet " 1 cord foot, c. ft.
8 cord feet, or ⎫
128 cubic feet ⎭ " 1 cord of wood, C.

1. How many cubic feet in 2 cubic yards? in 3 cubic yards?
2. How many cubic feet in 2 perch of stone? in 4 perch? in 6 perch?
3. How many cord feet in 3 cords of wood? in 7 cords? in 9 cords?
4. How many cord feet in 120 cubic feet of wood? in 200 cubic feet?
5. How many cords in 24 cord feet? in 56 cord feet?

---

33. TABLE OF LIQUID MEASURE.

4 gills (gi.) make 1 pint, pt.
2 pints " 1 quart, qt.
4 quarts " 1 gallon, gal.
31½ gallons " 1 barrel, bar.
2 barrels, or 63 gallons " 1 hogshead, hhd.

1. How many gills in 4 pints? in 6 pints? in 10 pints?
2. How many pints in 3 quarts? in 8 quarts? in 1 gallon? in 3 gallons?
3. How many gills in 4 quarts? in 6 quarts? in 8 quarts?
4. How many quarts in 3 gallons? how many pints? how many gills in 3 quarts? in 1 gallon and 2 quarts?

5. How many gills in 2 gallons 2 qts. ?
6. How many quart cups could be filled from a 10 gallon keg of wine? how many pint bottles?
7. In 48 gills, how many pints? quarts?
8. How many gallons in 64 gills? in 96 gills?
9. How many quarts in 56 pints? gallons?
10. In 10 gallons, how many quarts? pints? gills?
11. What will be the cost of 6 gallons of burning fluid, at 15 cents a quart?
12. If a pint of molasses cost 7 cents, what will a gallon cost?
13. If one gallon of oil cost 90 cents, what will 3 gallons and 2 quarts cost?
14. If you should draw 10 gallons and 8 quarts from a hogshead of molasses, how much would remain?

---

34. Table of Dry Measure.

2 pints (pt.)	make	1 quart,	qt.
8 quarts	"	1 peck,	pk.
4 pecks	"	1 bushel	bu.

1. How many pints in 1 peck? in 2 pks. 4 qts. ?
2. How many quarts in 1 bu. 2 pks. ?
3. In 2 bu. 1 pk. 6 qts. how many quarts?
4. In 64 quarts how many pecks? bushels?
5. In 80 pints how many pecks?
6. At 3 cents a pint, what will be the cost of one peck of chestnuts?
7. If one bushel of hickory nuts cost 160 cents, what will be the cost of 6 quarts?
8. Bought 2 pecks of cranberries for 96 cents, and sold them for 5 cents a pint; how much was the gain?

35.   TABLE OF TIME.

60 seconds (sec.)	make	1 minute,	m.
60 minutes	"	1 hour,	hr.
24 hours	"	1 day,	d.
7 days	"	1 week,	w.
12 calendar months	"	1 year,	yr.
365 days	"	1 common year,	yr.
366 days	"	1 leap year,	yr.
100 years	"	1 century,	C.

The divisions of the year, the names of the months, and the number in each, are shown in the following table : —

Winter.	1st	month,	January	has	31	days.
	2d	"	February	"	28*	"
Spring.	3d	"	March	"	31	"
	4th	"	April	"	30	"
	5th	"	May	"	31	"
Summer.	6th	"	June	"	30	"
	7th	"	July	"	31	"
	8th	"	August	"	31	"
Autumn.	9th	"	September	"	30	"
	10th	"	October	"	31	"
	11th	"	November	"	30	"
Winter.	12th	"	December	"	31	"

The following lines will help to remember the number of days in each month : —

> Thirty days hath September,
> April, June, and November;
>   All the rest have thirty-one,
>   Save February, which alone
> Hath twenty-eight; and one day more
> We add to it, one year in four.

* In leap-year, 29.

1. How many seconds in 2 minutes? in 5 minutes?
2. How many seconds in 10 minutes? in 20 minutes?
3. How many seconds in 1 hour? in 2 hours?
4. How many minutes in 3 hours? in 5 hours?
5. How many hours in 2 days? in 3 days?
6. In 2 days and 12 hours how many hours?
7. In 6 weeks how many days? in 9 weeks?
8. How many weeks in 49 days? in 84 days?
9. How many weeks and days in 75 days? in 90 days?
10. How many hours in 3 days 10 hours?
11. In 36 months how many years? in 84 months?
12. How many days from January 1st to March 10th, inclusive?
13. How many days from April 10th to the 15th of June?

---

36.   Miscellaneous Table.

12 units	make	1 dozen.
12 dozen	"	1 gross.
12 gross	"	1 great gross.
20 units	"	1 score.
24 sheets of paper	"	1 quire.
20 quires	"	1 ream.
56 pounds	"	1 bushel of corn.
60 pounds	"	1 bushel of wheat.
196 pounds	"	1 barrel of flour.
200 pounds	" {	1 barrel of beef, pork, or fish.

1. What cost 1 ream of paper, at 20 cents a quire?
2. What cost 3 dozen lemons, at 3 cents apiece?
3. What cost 2 gross of pens, at 5 cents a dozen?
4. At 7 dollars a hundred pounds, what will 2 barrels of pork cost?

CHAPTER VI.

FRACTIONS.

37. 1. WHAT is understood by *one half, one third, one fourth, one fifth,* &c.?

ANS. When a number or thing, as a unit or an apple, is divided into *two* equal parts, each of the parts is called *one half;* when into *three* equal parts, each of the parts is called *one third; two* of the parts are called *two thirds,* &c.

2. How many halves in 1?

3. How many thirds in 1?

4. If a peach be divided into 2 equal parts, what is each part called?

5. If an orange be divided into 3 equal parts, what are the parts called?

6. How many halves in 4?

ANALYSIS. *Since in* 1 *there are* 2 *halves, in* 4 *there are* 4 *times* 2 *halves, or* 8 *halves. Therefore there are* 8 *halves in* 4.

7. How many halves in 5? in 6?

8. How many halves in 7? in 7 and 1 half?

9. How many thirds in 3? in 4? in 5?

10. How many thirds in 7? in 8? in 9?

11. How many thirds in 6 and 1 third? in 6 and 2 thirds?

12. How many halves in 5? how many thirds?

13. How many halves in 10 and 1 half?

14. How many thirds in 9 and 2 thirds?

15. In 8 halves how many whole things?

ANALYSIS. *Since in* 2 *halves there is one whole thing, in* 8 *halves there are as many whole things as* 2, *the number of halves in* 1, *is contained times in* 8, *which is* 4 *times. Therefore, in* 8 *halves there are* 4 *whole things.*

16. How many whole things in 12 halves? in 16 halves? in 24 halves?

17. How many whole things in 9 thirds? in 18 thirds?

18. How many whole things in 10 halves? in 12 thirds? in 21 thirds? in 20 halves?

19. How many half bushels in 3 bushels and 1 half?

20. John gave 6 peaches to his 2 brothers; what part of them did each have?

21. What is 1 half of 6?

ANALYSIS. *It is that number which taken 2 times will make 6; 2 times 3 is 6. Therefore 3 is 1 half of 6.*

22. What is 1 third of 9? of 18? of 27? of 36?

23. What is 1 half of 8? of 12? of 18? of 22?

24. How can you take 1 half of an orange? 1 third?

25. How can you take 2 thirds of an apple?

26. William had 30 new pennies, and John had 1 half as many; how many had John?

27. If a pound of candles cost 15 cents, what will 1 third of a pound cost? 2 thirds?

28. George is 12 years old, and Mary is 2 thirds as old as he; how old is Mary?

29. If a barrel of flour cost 10 dollars, and a barrel of cider 1 half as much, what is the cost of the cider?

30. If 3 tons of hay cost 27 dollars, what part of 27 dollars will 1 ton cost? 2 tons?

31. A boy, having 33 cents, spent 2 thirds of them; how many had he left?

32. Edwin gave 2 peaches and 1 half to his sister, and 1 peach and 1 half to his brother; how many peaches did he give to both?

33. A farmer, having 44 sheep, sold 1 half of them; how many had he left?

38. 1. What do you understand by 1 fourth? 3 fourths?

2. What do you understand by 1 fifth? 2 fifths? 3 fifths? 4 fifths?

3. What do you understand by 1 sixth? 3 sixths? 5 sixths?

4. How can you take 1 fourth of any thing? 1 sixth?

5. How can you take 3 fourths of any thing? 3 fifths?

6. How many fifths in 1? in 4? in 6?

7. How many fourths in 1? in 2 and 3 fourths?

8. How many sixths in 2? in 3 and 4 sixths?

9. In 4 and 5 sixths how many sixths?

10. In 8 and 3 fourths how many fourths?

11. In 7 and 4 fifths how many fifths?

12. Which is greater, 1 fourth or 1 fifth? 1 fifth or 1 sixth?

13. How many times 1 in 8 fourths? in 16 fourths?

14. How many times 1 in 15 fifths? in 25 fifths?

15. How many times 1 in 24 sixths? in 36 sixths?

16. What is 1 fourth of 12? of 20? of 28?

17. What is 1 sixth of 18? of 30? of 42?

18. What is 1 fourth of 32? of 40? of 48?

19. What is 1 fifth of 10? of 20? of 50?

20. What is 1 sixth of 36? 2 sixths? 5 sixths?

21. What is 1 fifth of 40? 3 fifths? 4 fifths?

22. What is 3 fourths of 16? of 24?

23. What is 2 fifths of 10? of 25?

24. What is 3 sixths of 30? 5 sixths of 42?

25. If a ton of hay cost 12 dollars, what will 1 fourth of a ton cost? 2 fourths? 3 fourths?

26. If 5 bushels of apples cost 90 cents, what part of 90 cents will 1 bushel cost? 2 bushels? 3 bushels?

27. When coal is 6 dollars a ton, what part of a ton can be bought for 1 dollar? for 2 dollars? for 5 dollars?

28. Bought a piece of land for 45 dollars; what is 1 fifth of it worth? 2 fifths? 3 fifths?

29. If you pay 30 dollars for one month's labor, what do you pay for 1 fifth of a month? for 1 sixth? for 5 sixths? for 4 fifths?

30. A man divided 48 cents equally among 6 beggars; what part of the whole did each beggar receive? what part did 2 receive? 3? 4? 5?

31. If in a basket of 54 eggs 1 sixth are bad, how many are good?

32. If a man earn 15 dollars a week, and spend 2 fifths of it, how much does he save?

33. A drover, having 60 sheep, sold 1 fourth of them at one time, and 1 fifth at another; how many had he left?

34. Rollin had 18 marbles, and gave 2 sixths of them to Martin; how many did he give Martin, and how many did he keep for himself?

35. If Harry bought 6 pounds of coffee for 1 dollar, what part of 1 dollar did 1 pound cost? 2 pounds? 3 pounds? 4 pounds?

36. When tea is 5 shillings a pound, what part of a pound can be bought for 1 shilling? 2 shillings? 3 shillings? 4 shillings?

37. If a barrel of pork cost 15 dollars, what will 2 thirds of it cost? 3 fifths?

38. A gentleman is 60 years old, and his wife is 4 fifths as old; how old is she?

39. Andrew is 18 years old, and his sister, Jane, is 5 sixths as old; how old is Jane?

40. Paid 36 dollars for 1 acre of land; what is 1 sixth of it worth? 3 sixths? 1 fourth? 3 fourths?

41. If you divide a barrel of flour equally among 5 poor families, what part of the barrel will 1 family receive? 2 families? 3 families? 4 families? 5 families?

39. 1. What do you understand by 1 seventh? 3 sevenths? 4 sevenths? 5 sevenths?

2. What is meant by 1 eighth? 5 eighths? 1 ninth? 3 ninths? 5 ninths? 7 ninths?

3. What is meant by 3 tenths? 9 tenths? 5 twelfths? 11 twentieths?

4. How many ninths in a unit, or whole thing? how many tenths? how many elevenths? how many twelfths? how many twentieths?

5. How many times 1 in 14 sevenths? in 32 eighths? in 45 ninths?

6. How many times 1 in 70 tenths? in 44 elevenths? in 30 fifteenths? in 80 twentieths?

7. What is 1 seventh of 42? of 63? of 84?

8. What is 1 eighth of 24? of 56? of 64?

9. What is 1 ninth of 36? 3 ninths? 7 ninths?

10. What are 3 tenths of 50? of 60? of 90?

11. What is 1 twelfth of 72? 5 twelfths? 7 twelfths?

12. What is 1 twentieth of 60? 14 twentieths?

13. How many times 1 in 19 eighths? in 40 ninths? in 65 twelfths?

14. How many times 1 in 25 sevenths? in 56 tenths? in 52 elevenths?

15. In 3 and 5 sevenths how many sevenths?

16. In 6 and 3 eighths how many eighths?

17. In 8 and 7 ninths how many ninths?

18. In 9 and 3 twelfths how many twelfths?

19. In 7 and 9 tenths how many tenths?

20. If 10 pounds of sugar cost 80 cents, what part of 80 cents will 3 pounds cost? 5 pounds?

21. If a man earn 72 dollars in 1 month, how much will he earn in 1 fourth of a month? 5 sixths? 4 ninths? 7 eighths? 5 twelfths?

22. What is the difference between 7 eighths of 64 and 5 ninths of 81?

23. What will 5 eighths of a bushel of chestnuts cost at 10 cents a quart?

24. What will be the cost of 4 sevenths of 14 dozen of eggs at 11 cents a dozen?

25. If James has 108 cents, and Henry has 7 twelfths as many and 20 cents more, how many cents has Henry?

26. What will be the cost of 1 ninth of a hogshead of molasses at 12 cents a quart?

27. Menzo, having 48 dollars, gave 1 sixteenth of his money for a hat, 3 eighths for a coat, and 3 twelfths for some books and a quarter's tuition; how many dollars had he left?

28. A man bought a horse for 120 dollars; he gave 7 tenths as much for a carriage as he paid for the horse, and 3 sevenths as much for a harness as he paid for the carriage; how much did the whole cost him?

29. If a man put 200 dollars at interest, and receive 3 twentieths of it annually for its use, how many dollars does he receive?

30. If a vessel sail 12 miles an hour, how many times 9 miles will she sail in 3 eighths of a day?

31. Abel has 49 marbles, and Alonzo has 6 sevenths as many wanting 10; how many has Alonzo?

32. A man, having 300 cedar posts, sold 2 fifths of them to A, 1 sixth to B, 3 tenths to C, and 40 posts to D; how many had he left?

33. What will be the cost of a gold watch weighing 1 third of a pound at 1 dollar a pennyweight?

34. What will be the cost of 3 eighths of 2 gallons of wine at 40 cents a pint?

35. A grocer bought 27 dozen of eggs for 240 cents, and sold 5 ninths of them for 12 cents a dozen, and the remainder for 10 cents a dozen; how much did he gain by the operation?

40.   1. 9 is 1 fourth of what number ? -

ANALYSIS.   *9 is 1 fourth of 4 times 9 ; 4 times 9 is*
36. *Therefore 9 is 1 fourth of 36.*

2.   7 is 1 fifth of what number ?
3. 10 is 1 eighth of what number ?
4. 12 is 1 tenth of what number ?
5. 20 is 1 half of what number ?
6. 15 is 1 fourth of what number ?
7. 30 is 1 sixth of what number ?
8.   9 is 1 twelfth of what number ?
9.   5 is 1 twentieth of what number ?
10. 11 is 1 seventh of what number ?
11. 9 times 4, and 3 fourths of 4 are how many ?
12. 6 times 9, and 7 ninths of 9 are how many ?
13. 10 times 12, and 5 twelfths of 12 are how many ?
14. 14 times 2, and 1 half of 2 are how many ?
15. 8 times 11, and 7 elevenths of 11 are how many ?
16. 5 times 20, and 13 twentieths of 20 are how
many ?
17. 64 are how many times 8 ? 5 ? 12 ?
18. 47 are how many times 9 ? 10 ? 8 ? 6 ?
19. 81 are how many times 8 ? 9 ? 11 ? 12 ?
20. 35 are how many times 7 ? 6 ? 8 ? 9 ?
21. 75 are how many times 5 ? 6 ? 7 ? 9 ? 25 ?
22. 3 fourths of 16 are how many times 6 ?

ANALYSIS.   *3 fourths of 16 are as many times 6 as 6*
is contained times in 3 times ¼ of 16 ; 1 fourth of 16
is 4, and 3 times 4 is 12 ; 6 is contained in 12, 2 times.
Therefore 3 fourths of 16 are 2 times 6.

23. 6 tenths of 100 are how many times 5 ?
24. 5 twelfths of 72 are how many times 3 ? 4 ?
6 ? 8 ?
25. 7 ninths of 63 — 3 eighths of 24 are how
many times 4 ? 5 ? 6 ? 7 ? 8 ?
26. 11 twentieths of 80 + 7 fifteenths of 45 are
how many times 6 ? 7 ? 9 ? 12 ? 13 ?

41. ·1. If 1 fourth of a yard of cloth cost 12 cents, what will 1 yard cost?

ANALYSIS. *If* 1 *fourth of a yard cost* 12 *cents,* 4 *fourths, or* 1 *yard, will cost* 4 *times* 12 *cents ;* 4 *times* 12 *cents are* 48 *cents. Therefore, if* 1 *fourth of a yard cost* 12 *cents,* 1 *yard will cost* 48 *cents.*

2. If 1 fifth of a pound of tea cost 10 cents, what will 1 pound cost?

3. If 1 third of a gallon of molasses cost 20 cents, what will 1 gallon cost?

· 4. 20 is 1 third of what number?

5. 10 is 1 fifth of what number?

6. If 1 half of a cord of wood cost 2 dollars, what will 1 cord cost? what will 2 cords cost?

7. A man gave 2 shillings for his dinner, which was 1 twelfth of all the money he had ; how much money had he?

8. A drover sold some sheep, and gained by the sale 15 dollars, which was 1 fourth of what the sheep cost him ; what was the cost of the sheep?

9. If 1 sixth of a ton of hay cost 3 dollars, what will 3 sixths cost? 5 sixths? 1 ton?

10. If a man can walk 6 miles in 1 eighth of a day, how far can he walk in 1 day? in 2 days? in 3 days?

11. James had 40 plums, and divided 1 fourth of them equally among 5 of his companions; how many did he give to each?

12. 6 is 1 eighth of what number?

13. 15 is 1 fifth of what number?

14. 40 is 1 third of what number?

15. 1 fourth of 40 is how many times 5 ? 7 ?

16. 1 sixth of 90 is how many times 4 ? 5 ? 6 ?

17. I have 16 dollars, which is 1 third of what I paid for 12 sheep; how much did I pay a head?

18. A man plowed 36 acres of his farm; 3 fourths of this was just equal to 1 third of the whole number of acres in his farm; how many acres in his farm?

19. A pole stands 12 feet in the water, which is 1 fifth of the length of the pole; how long is the pole?

20. Bought a watch and chain; for the chain I gave 15 dollars, which was 1 fourth of what I paid for the watch; what did they both cost me?

21. If 1 twelfth of an acre of land cost 5 dollars, what will 2 acres cost?

---

42. 1. If 3 fourths of a barrel of flour cost 6 dollars, what will one barrel cost?

ANALYSIS. *If 3 fourths of a barrel of flour cost 6 dollars, 1 barrel will cost 4 times 1 third of 6 dollars; 1 third of 6 dollars are 2 dollars, and 4 times 2 dollars are 8 dollars. Therefore, &c.*

2. If 4 fifths of a barrel of ale cost 8 dollars, what will 1 barrel cost?

3. If 5 ninths of a month's wages amount to 25 dollars, what will a month's wages amount to? 2 months'?

4. What will 1 barrel of flour cost, if 5 sevenths of a barrel cost 10 dollars?

5. Sold a cow for 25 dollars, which was 5 fourths of what she cost me; what did she cost me?

6. Bought 4 barrels of vinegar at 6 dollars a barrel, which was but 3 ninths of its real value; what was its real value per barrel?

7. A speculator bought some pork for 90 dollars, which was 9 elevenths of what he sold it for; how much did he gain?

5

8. A tailor bought two pieces of cloth, the shorter piece containing 24 yards; 5 eighths the number of yards in the shorter piece is 20 yards less than the number of yards in the longer piece; how many yards in both pieces?

9. If 7 tenths of an acre of land yield 28 bushels of wheat, what will 1 acre yield? what will 3 acres yield?

10. 16 is 4 fifths of what number?

ANALYSIS. 16 *is* 4 *fifths of* 5 *times* 1 *fourth of* 16; 1 *fourth of* 16 *is* 4, *and* 5 *times* 4 *is* 20. *Therefore,* 16 *is* 4 *fifths of* 20.

11. 25 is 5 eighths of what number?
12. 14 is 7 twelfths of what number?
13. 9 is 3 tenths of what number?
14. 12 is 4 fifteenths of what number?
15. 20 is 2 sevenths of what number?
16. 18 is 6 elevenths of what number?
17. 21 is 3 halves of what number?
18. 72 is 9 eighths of what number?
19. 40 is 10 elevenths of what number?
20. 36 is 12 twentieths of what number?
21. 42 is 7 fifths of what number?
22. 5 sixths of 24 is 2 thirds of what number?

ANALYSIS. 5 *sixths of* 24 *is* 2 *thirds of* 3 *times* 1 *half of* 5 *times* 1 *sixth of* 24; 1 *sixth of* 24 *is* 4, *and* 5 *times* 4 *is* 20; 1 *half of* 20 *is* 10, *and* 3 *times* 10 *is* 30. *Therefore,* 5 *sixths of* 24 *is* 2 *thirds of* 30.

23. 3 fourths of 16 is 6 sevenths of what number?
24. 4 fifths of 30 is 8 elevenths of what number?
25. 6 fourths of 28 is 7 ninths of what number?
26. 9 twelfths of 60 is 5 thirds of what number?
27. 8 ninths of 18 is 1 fourth of what number?
28. 11 fifteenths of 45 is 3 halves of what number?

29. 6 tenths of 100 is 5 twelfths of what number?

30. 3 twentieths of 80 is 2 sixteenths of what number?

31. 9 eighths of 64 is 8 fifths of what number?

32. Of a certain farm, 36 acres are woodland, and 5 sixths of the woodland is 3 fifths of the number of acres of cleared land; how many acres of cleared land, and how many acres does the farm contain?

33. Mr. Smith gave 5 sevenths of all the money he had for a horse; he then paid 12 dollars for a saddle and bridle, which was 3 fourths of all the money he had left; how much money had he at first?

34. A person, being asked his age, answered that if he were twice as old, 1 third of his age would be 20 years; how old was he?

---

43. A FRACTION is one or more of the equal parts of a unit. Fractions are expressed by figures in the following manner, viz.:—

$\frac{1}{2}$, one half.　　　$\frac{2}{3}$, two thirds.
$\frac{1}{3}$, one third.　　$\frac{3}{4}$, three fourths,
$\frac{1}{4}$, one fourth.　$\frac{7}{8}$, seven eighths.
$\frac{1}{5}$, one fifth.　　$\frac{9}{10}$, nine tenths.
$\frac{1}{6}$, one sixth.　　$\frac{11}{12}$, eleven twelfths.
$\frac{1}{7}$, one seventh.　$\frac{13}{20}$, thirteen twentieths.
$\frac{1}{8}$, one eighth.　$4\frac{1}{7}$, four and 1 seventh.
$\frac{1}{10}$, one tenth.　$9\frac{5}{8}$, nine and 5 eighths, &c.

1. The number below the short horizontal line is called the *denominator*.

2. The number above the line is called the *numerator*.

3. The *denominator* shows into how many parts the whole thing is divided.

4. The *numerator* shows how many of these parts are taken or used.

5. A *proper fraction* is one whose *numerator* is *less* than the denominator; its value is *less* than a unit.

6. An *improper fraction* is one whose *numerator* is *equal to*, or *greater*, than the denominator; its value is *equal to*, or *greater*, than a unit.

7. A *mixed number* is a whole number joined with a fraction.

8. What kind of a fraction is $\frac{3}{4}$? What is the 4 called? What does it show?

9. In the fraction $\frac{3}{4}$, what is the 3 called? What does it show?

10. Into how many equal parts must a thing be divided to produce the fraction $\frac{4}{5}$? how many of these parts must be taken?

11. What kind of a fraction is $\frac{7}{4}$? Why?

12. What kind of a number is $6\frac{2}{3}$? Why?

13. How would you obtain $\frac{7}{8}$ of any thing?

14. How would you obtain $\frac{5}{6}$ of any thing?

15. How many times $\frac{1}{4}$ in 6?

ANALYSIS. *Since in* 1 *there are* 4 *times* $\frac{1}{4}$, *or* $\frac{4}{4}$, *in* 6 *there are* 6 *times* $\frac{4}{4}$, *or* $\frac{24}{4}$. *Therefore there are* 24 *times* $\frac{1}{4}$ *in* 6.

16. How many times $\frac{1}{3}$ in 4? in 8? in 9? in 12?

17. How many times $\frac{1}{5}$ in 3? in 5? in 7? in 8?

18. How many times $\frac{1}{8}$ in 2? in 4? in 5? in 7?

19. How many times $\frac{1}{12}$ in 5? in 6? in 7? in 9?

20. How many times $\frac{1}{20}$ in 3? in 4? in 6? in 7?

21. How many times $\frac{1}{6}$ in $3\frac{2}{6}$? in $4\frac{3}{6}$? in $7\frac{5}{6}$?

22. How many times $\frac{1}{7}$ in $2\frac{4}{7}$? in $5\frac{2}{7}$? in $6\frac{6}{7}$?

23. How many times $\frac{1}{10}$ in $5\frac{3}{10}$? in $7\frac{1}{10}$? in $8\frac{7}{10}$?

24. In $12\frac{1}{3}$ how many thirds?
25. In $7\frac{4}{5}$ how many fifths?
26. In $10\frac{3}{8}$ how many eighths?
27. In $9\frac{7}{12}$ how many twelfths?
28. In $15\frac{3}{4}$ how many fourths?
29. Reduce $20\frac{2}{3}$ to an improper fraction.
30. Reduce $8\frac{7}{9}$ to an improper fraction.
31. Reduce $7\frac{1}{12}$ to an improper fraction.
32. Reduce $8\frac{7}{9}$ to an improper fraction.
33. Reduce $25\frac{3}{4}$ to an improper fraction.
34. How do you reduce a whole number to a fraction having a required denominator?
35. How do you change a mixed number to an improper fraction?

---

44. 1. In $\frac{16}{4}$ how many times 1?

ANALYSIS. *Since $\frac{4}{4}$ equal 1, $\frac{16}{4}$ are as many times 1 as $\frac{4}{4}$ are contained times in $\frac{16}{4}$; $\frac{4}{4}$ are contained in $\frac{16}{4}$, 4 times. Therefore $\frac{16}{4}$ are 4 times 1, or 4.*

2. In $\frac{25}{5}$ how many times 1?
3. In $\frac{42}{6}$ how many times 1?
4. In $\frac{72}{9}$ how many times 1?
5. In $\frac{120}{12}$ how many times 1?
6. In $\frac{90}{15}$ how many times 1?
7. In $\frac{100}{5}$ how many times 1?
8. How many times 1 in $\frac{24}{10}$? in $\frac{36}{10}$? in $\frac{64}{10}$?
9. How many times 1 in $\frac{32}{8}$? in $\frac{45}{7}$? in $\frac{70}{9}$?
10. How many times 1 in $\frac{60}{4}$? in $\frac{48}{5}$? in $\frac{72}{11}$?
11. How many times 1 in $\frac{125}{30}$? in $\frac{150}{20}$? in $\frac{148}{12}$?
12. How many times 1 in $\frac{116}{9}$? in $\frac{205}{40}$? in $\frac{125}{5}$?
13. How many times 1 in $\frac{90}{7}$? in $\frac{108}{11}$? in $\frac{49}{3}$?
14. How many times 1 in $\frac{96}{26}$? in $\frac{114}{12}$? in $\frac{100}{30}$?

15. How many times 1 in $\frac{75}{50}$? in $\frac{84}{75}$? in $\frac{112}{50}$?

16. How do you reduce an improper fraction to a whole or mixed number?

17. Reduce $\frac{45}{25}$ to an equivalent whole number.

18. Reduce $\frac{104}{20}$ to an equivalent mixed number.

19. Reduce $\frac{84}{9}$ to an equivalent mixed number.

20. Reduce $\frac{70}{6}$ to an equivalent mixed number.

21. Express the value of $\frac{120}{60}$ in a whole number.

22. Express the value of $\frac{200}{150}$ in a mixed number.

23. Express the value of $\frac{95}{3}$ in a mixed number.

------

45.   1. In $\frac{2}{3}$ of 1, how many sixths?

ANALYSIS. *Since in* 1 *there are* $\frac{6}{6}$, *in* $\frac{2}{3}$ *of* 1, *there are* 2 *times* $\frac{1}{3}$ *of* $\frac{6}{6}$; $\frac{1}{3}$ *of* $\frac{6}{6}$ *is* $\frac{2}{6}$, *and* 2 *times* $\frac{2}{6}$ *are* $\frac{4}{6}$. *Therefore, &c.*

2. In $\frac{1}{5}$ of 1 how many tenths?

3. In $\frac{3}{4}$ of 1 how many twentieths?

4. In $\frac{1}{8}$ of 1 how many fortieths?

5. In $\frac{4}{5}$ of 1 how many tenths?

6. In $\frac{7}{8}$ of 1 how many sixteenths?

7. In $\frac{3}{7}$ of 1 how many twenty-firsts?

8. In $\frac{7}{9}$ of 1 how many thirty-sixths?

9. In $\frac{5}{6}$ of 1 how many twelfths?

10. In $\frac{3}{5}$ of 1 how many twenty-fifths?

11. In $\frac{5}{12}$ of 1 how many sixtieths?

12. In $\frac{1}{3}$ of 1 how many eighteenths?

13. In $\frac{7}{10}$ of 1 how many fortieths?

14. In $\frac{9}{20}$ of 1 how many eightieths?

15. In $\frac{11}{15}$ of 1 how many thirtieths?

16. In $\frac{3}{4}$ of 1 how many eighths?

17. In $\frac{5}{6}$ of 1 how many fourteenths?

18. In $\frac{8}{9}$ of 1 how many twenty-sevenths ?
19. In $\frac{5}{8}$ of 1 how many fifty-sixths ?
20. In $\frac{4}{11}$ of 1 how many forty-fourths ?
21. In $\frac{11}{16}$ of 1 how many thirty-seconds ?
22. In $\frac{9}{40}$ of 1 how many eightieths ?
23. In $\frac{25}{30}$ of 1 how many ninetieths ?
24. In $\frac{15}{24}$ of 1 how many one hundred twentieths ?
25. How many sixths in $\frac{15}{18}$?

ANALYSIS. *Since in 1 there are* $\frac{18}{18}$, *in* $\frac{1}{6}$ *of 1 are* $\frac{1}{6}$ *of* $\frac{18}{18}$, *or* $\frac{3}{18}$; *and* $\frac{3}{18}$ *is contained in* $\frac{15}{18}$, 5 *times. Therefore in* $\frac{15}{18}$ *are 5 sixths.*

26. How many eighths in $\frac{9}{24}$? in $\frac{10}{16}$?
27. How many fourths in $\frac{15}{20}$? in $\frac{9}{12}$?
28. How many thirds in $\frac{20}{30}$? in $\frac{10}{24}$?
29. How many sevenths in $\frac{16}{28}$? in $\frac{12}{21}$?
30. How many twelfths in $\frac{28}{84}$? in $\frac{12}{24}$?
31. How many ninths in $\frac{21}{27}$? in $\frac{20}{45}$?
32. How many sixths in $\frac{35}{42}$? in $\frac{16}{48}$?
33. How many eighths in $\frac{32}{64}$? in $\frac{50}{80}$?
34. How many fourteenths in $\frac{16}{28}$? in $\frac{20}{56}$?
35. How many fifths in $\frac{30}{75}$? in $\frac{20}{50}$?
36. How many sevenths in $\frac{27}{63}$? in $\frac{24}{56}$?
37. How many fourths in $\frac{48}{64}$? in $\frac{18}{24}$?
38. How many sixths in $\frac{50}{60}$? in $\frac{12}{66}$?
39. How many halves in $\frac{56}{28}$? in $\frac{42}{12}$?
40. How many tenths in $\frac{24}{60}$? in $\frac{27}{90}$?
41. How many fifteenths in $\frac{21}{45}$? in $\frac{30}{75}$?
42. How many elevenths in $\frac{28}{44}$? in $\frac{16}{22}$?
43. How many sixteenths in $\frac{40}{64}$? in $\frac{15}{48}$?
44. How many twentieths in $\frac{36}{120}$? in $\frac{42}{100}$?
45. How many twenty-fourths in $\frac{48}{72}$? in $\frac{42}{144}$?

46. 1. Reduce $\frac{6}{12}$ to its lowest terms.

NOTE. A fraction is said to be in its lowest terms when no number greater than 1 will exactly divide both numerator and denominator.

2. Reduce $\frac{9}{18}$ to its lowest terms.
3. Reduce $\frac{16}{32}$ to its lowest terms.
4. Reduce $\frac{20}{30}$ to its lowest terms.
5. Reduce $\frac{18}{27}$ to its lowest terms.
6. Reduce $\frac{25}{60}$ to its lowest terms.
7. Reduce $\frac{28}{42}$ to its lowest terms.
8. Reduce $\frac{11}{33}$ to its lowest terms.
9. Reduce $\frac{25}{75}$ to its lowest terms.
10. Reduce $\frac{48}{72}$ to its lowest terms.
11. Reduce $\frac{36}{84}$ to its lowest terms.
12. Reduce $\frac{75}{100}$ to its lowest terms.
13. Reduce $\frac{45}{90}$ to its lowest terms.
14. Reduce $\frac{56}{48}$ to its lowest terms.
15. Reduce $\frac{31}{62}$ to its lowest terms.
16. Reduce $\frac{96}{108}$ to its lowest terms.
17. Reduce $\frac{120}{240}$ to its lowest terms.
18. Reduce $\frac{96}{120}$ to its lowest terms.
19. Reduce $\frac{56}{24}$ to its lowest terms.
20. Reduce $\frac{81}{37}$ to its lowest terms.
21. Reduce $\frac{12}{132}$ to its lowest terms.
22. Reduce $\frac{120}{80}$ to its lowest terms.
23. How do you reduce a fraction to its lowest terms?

REMARKS. 1. If the numerator be multiplied by any number, the value of the fraction will be multiplied as many times as there are units in the multiplier.

2. If the numerator be divided by any number, the value of the fraction will be divided as many times as there are units in the divisor.

3. If the denominator be multiplied by any number, the value of the fraction will be divided as many times as there are units in the multiplier.

47. Fractions are said to have a *common denominator* when their denominators are alike. Any number that can be divided by each of the denominators of the given fractions may be taken for the common denominator.

1. Reduce $\frac{1}{4}$ and $\frac{2}{3}$ to fractions having a common denominator.

ANALYSIS. *12 is exactly divisible by 4 and 3, and may therefore be taken for a common denominator. Since in 1 there are $\frac{12}{12}$, in $\frac{1}{4}$ of 1 there must be $\frac{1}{4}$ of $\frac{12}{12}$, or $\frac{3}{12}$, and in $\frac{2}{3}$ of 1 there must be $\frac{2}{3}$ of $\frac{12}{12}$, or $\frac{8}{12}$. Therefore $\frac{1}{4}$ and $\frac{2}{3}$ are equal to $\frac{3}{12}$ and $\frac{8}{12}$.*

2. Reduce $\frac{1}{3}$ and $\frac{4}{5}$ to fractions having a common denominator.

3. Reduce $\frac{3}{4}$ and $\frac{1}{6}$ to a common denominator.

4. Reduce $\frac{1}{2}$ and $\frac{6}{7}$ to a common denominator.

5. Reduce $\frac{2}{3}$ and $\frac{5}{9}$ to a common denominator.

6. Reduce $\frac{3}{8}$ and $\frac{1}{3}$ to a common denominator.

7. Reduce $\frac{3}{7}$ and $\frac{3}{5}$ to a common denominator.

8. Reduce $\frac{5}{6}$, $\frac{4}{9}$, and $\frac{1}{6}$ to a common denominator.

9. Reduce $\frac{3}{7}$, $\frac{1}{4}$, and $\frac{3}{14}$ to a common denominator.

10. Reduce $\frac{4}{15}$, $\frac{1}{12}$ and $\frac{1}{6}$ to a common denominator.

11. Reduce $\frac{1}{2}$, $\frac{5}{16}$ and $\frac{7}{8}$ to a common denominator.

12. Reduce $\frac{2}{3}$, $\frac{3}{4}$, $\frac{5}{6}$ and $\frac{7}{8}$ to a common denominator.

13. Reduce $\frac{3}{10}$, $\frac{7}{20}$ and $\frac{9}{30}$ to a common denominator.

14. Reduce $1\frac{1}{2}$, $2\frac{1}{4}$ and $\frac{5}{8}$ to a common denominator.

---

4. If the denominator be divided by any number, the value of the fraction will be multiplied as many times as there are units in the divisor.

5. If both numerator and denominator be multiplied by the same number, the value of the fraction will not be changed.

6. If both numerator and denominator be divided by the same number, the value of the fraction will not be changed.

48. 1. James has $\frac{2}{5}$ of a dollar, John $\frac{3}{5}$ of a dollar, and George $\frac{4}{5}$ of a dollar; how many fifths of a dollar have they all? how many dollars?

ANALYSIS. *They all have the sum of* $\frac{2}{5} + \frac{3}{5} + \frac{4}{5}$, *equal to* $\frac{10}{5}$ *dollars, equal to 2 dollars. Therefore, &c.*

2. Jane had $\frac{4}{7}$ of a dollar and her father gave her $\frac{2}{7}$ of a dollar more; how much had she then?

3. Austin buys a pair of skates for $\frac{7}{8}$ of a dollar, a pair of mittens for $\frac{3}{8}$ of a dollar, and a slate for $\frac{1}{8}$ of a dollar; what is the cost of all?

4. A grocer sold $\frac{1}{2}$ dozen eggs to one man, $\frac{1}{3}$ of a dozen to another, and $\frac{5}{6}$ of a dozen to another; how many dozen did he sell to all?

NOTE. Fractions having different denominators must be reduced to a common denominator before adding or subtracting.

5. Mary paid $\frac{3}{8}$ of a dollar for some ribbon, $\frac{5}{6}$ of a dollar for a pair of gloves and $\frac{1}{3}$ of a dollar for a pair of hose; what was the cost of the whole?

6. Sold $\frac{3}{5}$ of an acre of land to one man, $\frac{2}{3}$ to another and $\frac{7}{15}$ to another; how much was sold to all?

7. A laborer dug $\frac{1}{2}$ a rod of ditch the first hour, $\frac{3}{4}$ of a rod the second, $\frac{3}{5}$ the third and $\frac{7}{10}$ the fourth; how many rods did he dig in 4 hours?

8. A farmer sold $\frac{1}{3}$ of his grain to one man, $\frac{2}{5}$ to another, and $\frac{1}{6}$ to another; what part of his grain did he sell?

9. Henry paid $\frac{4}{9}$ of a dollar for a sled, $\frac{1}{2}$ a dollar for a kite and $\frac{1}{6}$ of a dollar for a string; what was the cost of the whole?

10. Emma paid $2\frac{1}{3}$ dollars for a dress, $1\frac{3}{4}$ dollars for a pair of shoes and $\frac{1}{3}$ of a dollar for some ribbon; what was the cost of the whole?

NOTE. Add the whole numbers and the fractions separately, and then unite their sums.

11. Milton saved $\frac{5}{8}$ of a dollar one week, $\frac{2}{3}$ of a dollar the next, $1\frac{5}{6}$ the next and $2\frac{1}{4}$ the next; how much did he save in 4 weeks?

12. Albert picked $2\frac{1}{4}$ bushels of apples from one tree, $3\frac{3}{7}$ from another and $3\frac{1}{2}$ from another; how many bushels did he pick from the 3 trees?

13. If it take $4\frac{1}{9}$ yards of cloth for a coat, $2\frac{1}{6}$ yards for a pair of pantaloons, and $\frac{7}{9}$ of a yard for a vest, how many yards of cloth will it take for the whole?

14. If a man walk $12\frac{5}{9}$ miles in the forenoon and $10\frac{1}{6}$ miles in the afternoon, how many miles does he walk during the day?

15. Harvey bought a sled for $62\frac{1}{4}$ cents and sold it for $12\frac{1}{2}$ cents more than he gave for it; how much did he receive for it?

16. Three men bought a horse. A paid $25\frac{7}{12}$ dollars, B paid $30\frac{7}{8}$ dollars and C paid $35\frac{5}{6}$ dollars; what was the cost of the horse?

17. If coal is worth $5\frac{7}{16}$ dollars a ton, and wood is worth $3\frac{5}{12}$ dollars a cord, what will be the cost of one ton of coal and two cords of wood?

18. Find the sum of $\frac{7}{12}$ and $\frac{3}{10}$.

19. Find the sum of $\frac{2}{3}$, $\frac{4}{5}$ and $\frac{1}{6}$.

20. Find the sum of $\frac{7}{8}$, $\frac{4}{3}$ and $\frac{5}{16}$.

21. Find the sum of $\frac{9}{20}$, $\frac{7}{10}$ and $\frac{3}{8}$.

22. Find the sum of $\frac{1}{2}$, $\frac{1}{3}$ and $\frac{1}{4}$.

23. Add together $\frac{6}{7}$, $\frac{1}{8}$ and $\frac{3}{14}$.

24. Add together $\frac{7}{30}$, $\frac{9}{10}$ and $\frac{4}{5}$.

25. Add together $\frac{7}{18}$, $\frac{4}{9}$, $\frac{5}{12}$ and $\frac{1}{6}$.

26. Add together $\frac{5}{14}$, $\frac{4}{7}$ and $\frac{3}{4}$.

27. Add together $\frac{4}{5}$, $\frac{1}{9}$, $\frac{2}{15}$ and $\frac{1}{3}$.

28. Add together $\frac{1}{2}$, $\frac{1}{3}$, $\frac{1}{4}$, $\frac{1}{5}$ and $\frac{1}{6}$.

29. What is the sum of $2\frac{1}{2}$ and $3\frac{1}{3}$?

30. What is the sum of $8\frac{3}{4}$ and $12\frac{1}{8}$?

31. What is the sum of $14\frac{1}{5}$, $10\frac{5}{6}$, and $5\frac{1}{2}$?

32. What is the sum of $7\frac{3}{12} + 15\frac{5}{6} + 10\frac{1}{4}$?

33. What is the sum of $25\frac{1}{3} + 13\frac{2}{6} + 5\frac{7}{18}$?

34. What is the sum of $6\frac{4}{9} + 7\frac{1}{7} + 4\frac{2}{3}$?

35. What is the sum of $\frac{9}{10} + 11\frac{1}{2} + 14\frac{1}{4} + 10\frac{1}{5}$?

36. What is the sum of $3\frac{7}{20} + 5\frac{7}{8} + \frac{3}{4} + 10\frac{1}{2}$?

37. What is the sum of $6 + 14\frac{5}{12} + 5\frac{11}{30} + \frac{4}{15}$?

38. What is the sum of $20 + 7\frac{5}{11} + 1\frac{11}{22}$?

---

49.   1. Amos having $\frac{5}{6}$ of a dollar, gave $\frac{2}{6}$ of a dollar to a beggar; how much had he left?

ANALYSIS. *He had left the difference between $\frac{5}{6}$ and $\frac{2}{6}$ of a dollar; $\frac{5}{6} - \frac{2}{6} = \frac{3}{6}$ of a dollar. Therefore, &c.*

2. Norman had $\frac{7}{8}$ of a bushel of peaches; he sold $\frac{3}{8}$ of a bushel; what part of a bushel had he left?

3. Nancy paid $\frac{5}{6}$ of a dollar for a geography and $\frac{4}{6}$ of a dollar for a philosophy; for which did she pay the more, and how much?

4. Two men own a piece of property together; one owns $\frac{3}{7}$ of it; how much does the other own?

5. When rye is worth $\frac{7}{6}$ of a dollar per bushel and corn is worth $\frac{5}{6}$ of a dollar, what is the difference in the price?

6. A grocer sells $\frac{1}{3}$ of a box of tea from a box $\frac{6}{7}$ full; what part of the whole box is left?

7. Henry can run $\frac{7}{8}$ of a mile in the same time that John can run $\frac{17}{20}$; which runs the farther, and · how much?

8. Parley gave $\frac{1}{3}$ of a dollar for a vest and $\frac{2}{6}$ of a dollar for a pair of shoes; what was the difference in the cost?

9. A gentleman, owning a boat, sold $\frac{5}{18}$ of it; how much of it did he still own?

10. If Robert earn $7\frac{3}{4}$ dollars a week and Herman earn $6\frac{1}{3}$ dollars a week, how much more than Herman does Robert earn?

11. Arthur gathered $10\frac{7}{8}$ quarts of chestnuts and sold $7\frac{5}{6}$ quarts; how many quarts had he left?

12. From a piece of cloth containing $12\frac{1}{2}$ yards, $5\frac{2}{3}$ yards were cut; how many yards remained?

13. If I put $15\frac{4}{5}$ dollars in the bank at one time, how much must I afterwards put in to make the sum 20 dollars?

14. From a hogshead of molasses, $9\frac{3}{7}$ gallons were drawn; how many gallons remained?

15. Edgar will be 14 years old $3\frac{5}{12}$ years hence; how old is he now?

16. From a jug of molasses containing 1 gallon, $\frac{7}{8}$ of a quart was used; how much was left?

17. If I buy a book for $\frac{5}{8}$ of a dollar, how much change must be returned to me for a 3 dollar bill?

18. A lady, having $18\frac{3}{5}$ dollars, bought a bonnet for $5\frac{3}{4}$ dollars; how much money had she left?

19. What is the difference between $\frac{5}{7}$ and $\frac{3}{8}$?

20. What is the difference between $\frac{1}{4}$ and $\frac{1}{5}$?

21. What is the difference between $\frac{9}{10}$ and $\frac{2}{3}$?

22. What is the difference between $1\frac{1}{2}$ and $\frac{3}{4}$?

23. What is the difference between $3\frac{2}{3}$ and $1\frac{1}{2}$?

24. What is the difference between $16\frac{5}{8}$ and $9\frac{1}{2}$?

25. What is the difference between 20 and $12\frac{1}{8}$?

26. How many are $\frac{1}{2} - \frac{4}{9}$?

27. How many are $4\frac{3}{7} - \frac{7}{9}$?

28. How many are $12 - 6\frac{9}{14}$?

29. How many are $36\frac{1}{2} - 24\frac{5}{8}$?

30. How many are $25\frac{1}{7} - 10\frac{7}{9}$?

31. How many are $16 - 9\frac{3}{4}$?

32. How many are $28 - 17\frac{3}{8}$?

50. 1. Mr. Smith sold $\frac{1}{3}$ of his estate to A, $\frac{1}{6}$ of it to B and $\frac{1}{4}$ to C; what part remained unsold?

2. A gambler lost in play $\frac{1}{3}$ and $\frac{1}{2}$ of his money; what part had he left?

3. A lady paid $\frac{1}{3}$ of her money for a bonnet, $\frac{1}{4}$ for a shawl and $\frac{1}{6}$ for a pair of gaiters; what part had she left?

4. A laborer worked 3 days for $1\frac{1}{3}$, $\frac{7}{8}$, and $1\frac{1}{2}$ dollars; had he received 2 dollars a day, how much more would he have received?

5. From a piece of calico containing $32\frac{3}{4}$ yards, two dress patterns were cut, one containing $10\frac{1}{4}$ yards and the other $12\frac{3}{8}$ yards; how many yards remained in the piece?

6. I deposited in the bank at one time $\$20\frac{1}{3}$, at another $\$15\frac{7}{8}$; how much more must I deposit to make the amount $\$50$?

7. Paid $\$6\frac{5}{8}$ for a barrel of flour, $\$5\frac{2}{3}$ for a ton of coal, and gave in payment a 10 dollar bill and a 5 dollar bill; how much change must be returned to me?

8. A merchant bought 5 barrels of flour, at $\$15$ a barrel, and paid $\$45\frac{3}{10}$ in goods and the remainder in cash; how much cash did he pay?

9. If you divide $\$80$ among three men, giving the first $\frac{1}{4}$ of it, and the second $\$35\frac{1}{6}$, what will the third receive?

10. A farmer, having 120 bushels of oats to sell, sold $15\frac{1}{2}$ bushels more than $\frac{1}{3}$ of them at one time, and 20 bushels less than $\frac{1}{2}$ of them at another time; how many bushels had he left?

11. Asaph gave $\frac{1}{6}$ of his money for a sled, $\frac{3}{7}$ for a cap, and had 39 cents left; how much had he at first?

12. Morgan is $10\frac{5}{8}$ years old, Myron is $9\frac{3}{4}$ years old, and the sum of their ages is $5\frac{2}{3}$ years more than Martin's age; how old is Martin?

13. James is $9\frac{1}{2}$ years old, and Lewis is $5\frac{1}{3}$ years less than twice as old as James; what is the difference in their ages?

14. A man, having $64, bought 3 cows; for the first cow he gave $\frac{1}{4}$ of it, for the second $\frac{2}{5}$ of it, and the remainder for the third; what was the cost of the third cow?

15. A grocer drew from a hogshead $20\frac{3}{4}$ gallons of molasses at one time, and $25\frac{7}{8}$ gallons at another; how many gallons remained?

16. What number must be taken from 36 that the remainder may be $7\frac{6}{7}$?

17. From what number must $9\frac{1}{6}$ be taken to leave $12\frac{3}{7}$?

18. What number must be added to $16\frac{9}{10}$ that the sum may be $25\frac{2}{3}$?

19. A person being asked his age, replied that if $4\frac{3}{4}$ years were added to $12\frac{1}{6}$ years, the sum would be $\frac{1}{2}$ his age; what was his age?

20. A person, undertaking a journey of 60 miles, traveled $\frac{1}{4}$ of the distance the first day, $\frac{1}{3}$ of the remainder the second day, and $\frac{3}{5}$ of the remainder the third day; how far from his place of destination was he at the close of the third day?

21. What is the difference between $17\frac{3}{4}$ and $5\frac{1}{2} + 6\frac{1}{3}$?

22. What is the difference between $25\frac{1}{5}$ and $11\frac{1}{4} + 7\frac{3}{5}$?

23. What is the difference between $9 + 12\frac{1}{5}$ and $8\frac{2}{5} + 4\frac{1}{7}$?

24. From $30\frac{1}{4}$ take $20\frac{1}{2} + 3\frac{7}{12}$.

25. From $40 - 10\frac{2}{3}$ take $7\frac{1}{4} + 5\frac{1}{6}$.

26. From $28\frac{1}{9}$ take $21\frac{1}{3} - 5\frac{4}{6}$.

27. From $\frac{3}{8} + \frac{1}{4} + \frac{2}{3}$ take $\frac{1}{4} + \frac{2}{6} + \frac{3}{12}$.

28. From $3 + \frac{6}{7} + \frac{2}{3}$ take $1\frac{7}{21}$.

51. 1. What will 5 pounds of tea cost at $\frac{3}{4}$ of a dollar a pound ?

ANALYSIS. *Since* 1 *pound cost* $\frac{3}{4}$ *of a dollar,* 5 *pounds, which are* 5 *times* 1 *pound, will cost* 5 *times* $\frac{3}{4}$, *or* $\frac{15}{4}$, *of a dollar, equal to* $3\frac{3}{4}$. *Therefore* 5 *pounds of tea, at* $\frac{3}{4}$ *of a dollar a pound, will cost* $3\frac{3}{4}$.

2. What cost 4 yards of linen at $\frac{5}{8}$ of a dollar a yard ?

3. When sugar is $\frac{1}{7}$ of a dollar a pound, what will 25 pounds cost ?

4. If $\frac{1}{5}$ of a pound of butter last a family 1 day, how many pounds will last them one week ?

5. What will be the cost of 10 peaches at $\frac{7}{8}$ of a cent apiece ?

6. If a man earn $\frac{9}{10}$ of a dollar a day, how much will he earn in 12 days ?

7. If 1 peck of pears cost $\frac{1}{5}$ of a dollar, what will 2 bushels cost ?

8. How many loaves of bread must you give to 8 beggars, if you give them $\frac{5}{7}$ of a loaf apiece ?

9. At $\frac{3}{5}$ of a dime a pound, what will 15 pounds of nails cost ?

10. What will 9 yards of silk cost at $\frac{11}{12}$ of a dollar a yard ?

11. George had $\frac{13}{20}$ of a dollar, and William had 8 times as much ; how much had William ?

12. If 1 horse eat $\frac{3}{7}$ of a ton of hay in a month, how much will 10 horses eat ?

13. How many are 9 times $\frac{7}{8}$? 12 times $\frac{8}{9}$? 14 times $\frac{4}{13}$? 20 times $\frac{6}{40}$?

14. If 1 man can reap $\frac{4}{9}$ of an acre of rye in a day, how much can 11 men reap ?

15. How many barrels of flour will be given to 9 poor families, if each receive $\frac{7}{16}$ of a barrel ?

16. How many are 12 times $\frac{7}{10}$? 16 times $\frac{5}{8}$?

17. Bought 6 bushels of corn at $\$\frac{5}{8}$ a bushel, and had $4 left; how much money had I at first?

18. If 1 quart of molasses cost $\$\frac{3}{16}$, what will 4 gallons cost at the same rate?

19. If a boy give each of his 4 companions $\frac{2}{8}$ of a quart of chestnuts, and have $4\frac{1}{8}$ quarts left, how many quarts had he at first?

20. How do you multiply a fraction by a whole number?

---

52. 1. If 1 box of raisins cost $\$2\frac{3}{4}$, what will 5 boxes cost?

ANALYSIS. *If 1 box of raisins cost $\$2\frac{3}{4}$, 5 boxes, which are 5 times 1 box, will cost 5 times $\$2\frac{3}{4}$; 5 times $\frac{3}{4}$ are $\frac{15}{4}$, or $\$3\frac{3}{4}$; 5 times $\$2$ are $\$10$; $\$3\frac{3}{4}$ added to $\$10$ are $\$13\frac{3}{4}$. Therefore, if 1 box of raisins cost $\$2\frac{3}{4}$, 5 boxes will cost $\$13\frac{3}{4}$.*

2. At $12\frac{1}{2}$ cents a pound, what will 9 pounds of butter cost?

3. At $\$6\frac{2}{3}$ a barrel, what will 7 barrels of flour cost?

4. How many bushels of grain will 15 bags hold, if they hold $2\frac{1}{5}$ bushels apiece?

5. What will be the cost of 12 pounds of rice, at $6\frac{1}{4}$ cents a pound?

6. What will 9 dozen of eggs cost at $11\frac{1}{2}$ cents a dozen?

7. What will 7 yards of cloth cost at $\$5\frac{7}{16}$ a yard?

8. If 1 barrel of fish cost $\$14\frac{3}{5}$, what will 6 barrels cost?

9. If 1 horse eat $3\frac{1}{7}$ tons of hay in 5 months, how many tons will 20 horses eat in the same time?

10. If 1 pint of wine cost $\$1\frac{1}{5}$, what will 1 gallon cost?

11. If 5 men can do a piece of work in 10⅔ days, how long will it take 1 man to do the same ?

12. If a grain of gold is worth 4½ cents, what is 1 pennyweight worth ?

13. A grocer sold 9 pounds of coffee at 12½ cents a pound, and 7 pounds of sugar at 8¾ cents a pound; low much did he receive for both ?

14. If it take 3⅝ yards of cloth for a coat, and 2¼ yards for a pair of pantaloons, how many yards will be required to make 3 of each ?

---

53. 1. If 1 pound of cheese cost 10 cents, what will 5⅜ pounds cost ?

ANALYSIS. *Since* 1 *pound cost* 10 *cents,* 5⅜ *pounds, which are* 5⅜ *times* 1 *pound, will cost* 5⅜ *times* 10 *cents ;* 5 *times* 10 *cents are* 50 *cents,* ⅜ *of* 10 *cents are* 3 *times* ⅛ *of* 10 *cents ;* ⅛ *of* 10 *cents is* 1¼ *cents, and* ⅜ *of* 10 *cents are* 3 *times* 1¼ *cents, or* 3¾ *cents, which added to* 50 *cents make* 53¾ *cents. Therefore, &c.*

2. If a horse travel 6 miles an hour, how far will he travel in 7⅔ hours ?

3. If a person's expenses be $12 a week, what will they be for 9¾ weeks ?

4. What will 4⅗ barrels of cider cost at $3 a barrel?

5. What will 10¾ pounds of honey cost at 12 cents a pound ?

6. What will 15⅔ bushels of potatoes cost at 6 shillings a bushel ?

7. If a pint of wine is worth 40 cents, what are 3⅝ pints worth ?

8. If a man can build 4 rods of wall in a day, how many rods can he build in 7⅚ days ?

9. If a barrel of flour last a family 6 weeks, how long will 4¼ barrels last them ?

10. If stage fare is 4 cents a mile, what will it cost to ride $20\frac{3}{4}$ miles.

11. If a merchant pay 12 shillings for 3 caps, and sell them for $6\frac{2}{3}$ shillings apiece, what is his gain?

12. Bought $9\frac{1}{2}$ yards of silk at 12 shillings a yard, and $12\frac{5}{8}$ pounds of tea at 7 shillings a pound; how much more did the silk cost than the tea?

13. If I buy $8\frac{4}{9}$ tons of coal, at $5 a ton, how much less than $50 will it cost?

14. A woman took $6\frac{5}{6}$ dozen eggs to market, which she sold for 12 cents a dozen; she received in payment $4\frac{4}{5}$ yards of calico at 10 cents a yard, $3\frac{1}{4}$ yards of ribbon at 8 cents a yard; how much was still her due?

15. If $\frac{7}{8}$ of a barrel of flour last a family 1 month, how many barrels will last 8 such families $6\frac{2}{3}$ months?

16. What is the product of $4\frac{1}{3}$ times 9 multiplied by 3?

17. What is the product of 5 times $3\frac{1}{5}$ multiplied by $2\frac{7}{8}$?

18. Multiply $4\frac{1}{2}$ times 10 by $\frac{2}{5}$ of 15.

19. Multiply $3\frac{1}{2}$ times 6 by $\frac{1}{7}$ of 24.

20. Multiply $4\frac{3}{5}$ by $\frac{3}{8}$ of 16.

21. Multiply 2 times $9\frac{1}{6}$ by $2\frac{1}{4}$ times 4.

22. Multiply 5 times $3\frac{7}{8}$ by $\frac{4}{5}$ of 15.

23. What is the sum of 8 times $7\frac{3}{10}$ and $4\frac{3}{8}$ times 12?

24. What is the sum of $6\frac{3}{8}$ times 11 and 12 times $5\frac{3}{4}$?

25. What is the difference between $4\frac{3}{4}$ times 10 and 3 times $9\frac{7}{8}$?

26. What is the difference between 7 times $8\frac{1}{3}$ and $10\frac{1}{2}$ times 5?

27. How many are $12\frac{3}{7}$ times 7? $9\frac{2}{3}$ times 10?

28. How many are $5\frac{3}{5}$ times 15? $3\frac{1}{8}$ times 40?

54. 1. A man, owning $\frac{1}{2}$ of a store, sold $\frac{1}{4}$ of his share; what part of the whole store did he sell?

ANALYSIS. *He sold $\frac{1}{4}$ of $\frac{1}{2}$ of the store. Since $\frac{1}{2}$ is equal to $\frac{4}{8}$, $\frac{1}{4}$ of $\frac{1}{2}$ is equal to $\frac{1}{4}$ of $\frac{4}{8}$, or $\frac{1}{8}$. Therefore, he sold $\frac{1}{8}$ of the store.*

2. James had $\frac{1}{4}$ of a dollar, and gave $\frac{1}{5}$ of it to a beggar; what part of a dollar did he give away?

3. A boy, having $\frac{1}{2}$ of a watermelon, gave away $\frac{1}{6}$ of what he had; what part of the whole melon did he give away?

4. If a yard of crape cost $\frac{1}{2}$ of a dollar, what will $\frac{1}{3}$ of a yard cost?

5. If I own $\frac{1}{3}$ of an acre of land, and sell $\frac{1}{6}$ of it, what part of an acre do I sell?

6. If a bushel of apples be worth $\frac{1}{2}$ of a dollar, what is $\frac{1}{5}$ of a bushel worth?

7. John is $\frac{1}{3}$ as old as his father, and Henry is $\frac{1}{7}$ as old as John? what part of his father's age is Henry's age?

8. A merchant, having $\frac{1}{7}$ of a hogshead of molasses, sold $\frac{1}{6}$ of what he had; what part of the whole hogshead did he sell, and what part had he left?

9. Homer bought $\frac{1}{2}$ a box of figs, and Robert $\frac{1}{2}$ as many; what part of a box did both buy?

10. C owned $\frac{1}{6}$ of a steamboat, and sold $\frac{1}{8}$ of his share; what part of the whole did he sell?

11. Mr. Jones, owning $\frac{1}{2}$ of a cotton mill, sold $\frac{1}{3}$ of his share to B, and B sold $\frac{1}{2}$ of his share to C; what part of the whole did each have after the division?

12. A cistern, being full of water, sprang a leak, and before it could be stopped $\frac{1}{2}$ of the water ran out, but $\frac{1}{3}$ as much ran in at the same time; what part of the cistern was emptied?

13. A poor man, having $\frac{1}{2}$ of a barrel of flour,

gave $\frac{1}{5}$ of it to a poor neighbor, who gave $\frac{1}{4}$ of his share to a poor woman; what part of a barrel had each then?

14. Andrew, having $\$\frac{3}{4}$, gave $\frac{3}{5}$ of it for a knife; what part of a dollar did he pay for his knife?

ANALYSIS. *He paid $\frac{3}{5}$ of $\frac{3}{4}$ of a dollar. 3 fifths of $\frac{3}{4}$ are 3 times 1 fifth of $\frac{3}{4}$. $\frac{1}{5}$ of $\frac{3}{4}$ is $\frac{3}{20}$, and $\frac{3}{5}$ of $\frac{3}{4}$ are 3 times $\frac{3}{20}$, or $\frac{9}{20}$. Therefore, &c.*

15. If a yard of cloth is worth $\$\frac{7}{8}$, what is $\frac{1}{4}$ of a yard worth?

16. Harriet, having $\frac{4}{5}$ of a yard of silk, gave $\frac{3}{4}$ of it to her sister; what part of a yard did she give away, and what part of a yard had she left?

17. A man, owning $\frac{6}{7}$ of a farm, sold $\frac{3}{5}$ of his share to his brother; what part of the farm did each own?

18. Hannah picked $\frac{9}{10}$ of a pailful of strawberries, and on her way home spilled $\frac{3}{5}$ of them; what part of a pailful had she left?

19. What will be the cost of $\frac{2}{3}$ of a bushel of beans at $\$\frac{8}{9}$ a bushel?

20. Jacob, having $\frac{4}{5}$ of a pound of candy, gave $\frac{1}{2}$ of it to Mary, and $\frac{1}{4}$ of it to Jane; what part of a pound had he left?

21. A keeper of a saloon bought a cask of ale; $\frac{1}{4}$ of it leaked out, $\frac{2}{3}$ of the remainder he sold, and what was left he kept for his own use; what part of the cask did he keep?

22. How do you multiply one fraction by another?

23. What is $\frac{1}{2}$ of $\frac{1}{2}$?   29. What is $\frac{1}{5}$ of $\frac{1}{4}$?

24. What is $\frac{1}{5}$ of $\frac{1}{2}$?   30. What is $\frac{1}{3}$ of $\frac{1}{4}$?

25. What is $\frac{1}{4}$ of $\frac{1}{3}$?   31. What is $\frac{1}{8}$ of $\frac{1}{6}$?

26. What are $\frac{4}{7}$ of $\frac{1}{3}$?   32. What is $\frac{1}{2}$ of $\frac{5}{8}$?

27. What are $\frac{8}{9}$ of $\frac{3}{4}$?   33. What are $\frac{3}{4}$ of $\frac{2}{3}$?

28. What are $\frac{4}{5}$ of $\frac{9}{11}$?   34. What are $\frac{7}{8}$ of $\frac{6}{10}$?

55. 1. At $\$8\frac{4}{5}$ a barrel, what will $\frac{3}{4}$ of a barrel of flour cost?

Analysis. *Since 1 barrel cost* $\$8\frac{4}{5}$, $\frac{3}{4}$ *of a barrel, which is 3 times* $\frac{1}{4}$, *will cost 3 times* $\frac{1}{4}$ *of* $\$8\frac{4}{5}$. $\frac{1}{4}$ *of* \$8 *is* \$2, *and* $\frac{1}{4}$ *of* $\$\frac{4}{5}$ *is* $\$\frac{1}{5}$, *which added to* \$2 *makes* $\$2\frac{1}{5}$. *3 times* \$2 *are* \$6, *and 3 times* $\frac{1}{5}$ *are* $\frac{3}{5}$, *which added to* \$6 *make* $\$6\frac{3}{5}$. *Therefore, &c.*

Or, $\$8\frac{4}{5}$ *are equal to* $\frac{44}{5}$, *and* $\frac{3}{4}$ *of* $\frac{44}{5} = \frac{33}{5}$, *or* $\$6\frac{3}{5}$.

2. At $\$6\frac{1}{4}$ a bushel, what will $\frac{2}{3}$ of a bushel of clover seed cost?

3. At $\$12\frac{5}{6}$ a ton, what will $\frac{5}{6}$ of a ton of hay cost?

4. If a man travel $24\frac{1}{2}$ miles in 1 day, how far will he travel in $\frac{1}{3}$ of a day?

5. What will $\frac{3}{5}$ of a barrel of beef cost, at $\$15\frac{3}{4}$ a barrel?

6. What will be the cost of $\frac{1}{4}$ of a cord of wood, if 1 cord cost $\$5\frac{1}{3}$?

7. At $10\frac{1}{2}$ shillings a day, how much can a man earn in $\frac{3}{4}$ of a day?

8. If a man can cut $3\frac{1}{2}$ acres of rye in 1 day, how much can he cut in $\frac{5}{9}$ of a day?

9. If I pay $\$6\frac{3}{5}$ for a jar of butter, what is $\frac{1}{4}$ of it worth?

10. Bought a horse for $\$75\frac{1}{2}$, and sold him for $\frac{4}{5}$ of what he cost; what was the loss?

11. What is $\frac{1}{3}$ of $14\frac{1}{2}$? of $20\frac{3}{4}$? of $13\frac{1}{5}$? of $18\frac{1}{3}$?

12. What are $\frac{2}{7}$ of $9\frac{3}{5}$? of $12\frac{4}{9}$? of $16\frac{2}{3}$? of $21\frac{1}{4}$?

13. What are $\frac{2}{3}$ of $21\frac{6}{7}$? $\frac{3}{5}$ of $32\frac{1}{6}$? $\frac{5}{6}$ of $23\frac{1}{2}$?

14. At $\$\frac{2}{3}$ a yard, what will $6\frac{1}{4}$ yards of flannel cost?

Analysis. *Since 1 yard costs* $\$\frac{2}{3}$, $6\frac{1}{4}$ *yards will cost* $6\frac{1}{4}$ *times* $\$\frac{2}{3}$. *6 times* $\$\frac{2}{3}$ *are* $\frac{12}{3}$ *or* \$4, *and* $\frac{1}{4}$ *of* $\frac{2}{3}$ *is* $\frac{2}{12}$, *or* $\$\frac{1}{6}$, *which added to* \$4 *makes* $\$4\frac{1}{6}$. *Therefore, &c.*

Or, $6\frac{1}{4}$ *are equal to* $\frac{25}{4}$, *and* $\frac{25}{4}$ *of* $\frac{2}{3}$ *are* $\frac{50}{12}$, *or* $\$4\frac{1}{6}$. *Therefore, &c.*

15. At $\$\frac{3}{4}$ a bushel, what will $8\frac{4}{5}$ bushels of peaches cost?

16. If a man hoe $\frac{1}{8}$ of an acre of corn in 1 day, how many acres can he hoe in $5\frac{2}{3}$ days?

17. If a vessel sail $12\frac{4}{9}$ miles in 1 hour, how far does she sail in $\frac{5}{6}$ of an hour?

18. If a man has $22\frac{3}{5}$ bushels of clover seed, and he sell $\frac{3}{4}$ of it, how much has he left?

19. What will $\frac{1}{3}$ of $\frac{1}{2}$ of 12 gallons of oil cost, at $\$\frac{7}{10}$ a gallon?

20. At $\$\frac{3}{7}$ a rod, what will it cost to dig $\frac{1}{2}$ of $\frac{3}{4}$ of 28 rods of ditch?

21. What will $4\frac{1}{2}$ yards of cloth cost at $\$2\frac{1}{4}$ a yard?

Note. Reduce the mixed numbers to improper fractions, and then proceed as in multiplying one fraction by another.

22. If you earn $8\frac{1}{2}$ shillings in 1 day, how much can you earn in $2\frac{2}{3}$ days?

23. What cost $2\frac{5}{6}$ dozen of eggs at $10\frac{1}{2}$ cents a dozen?

24. What will $3\frac{2}{3}$ yards of shalloon cost at $\$1\frac{3}{10}$ a yard?

25. If a man can do a job of work in $5\frac{4}{5}$ days, in what time can he do a job $1\frac{2}{3}$ times as large?

26. Clorinda is $7\frac{3}{4}$ years old, and Augusta is $\frac{5}{6}$ as old; how old is she?

27. A man paid $\$16\frac{2}{3}$ for a cow, and $2\frac{1}{2}$ times as much for a colt; how much did he pay for both?

28. What is the product of $3\frac{2}{3}$ times $9\frac{1}{4}$?

29. What is the product of $8\frac{1}{3}$ times $10\frac{3}{8}$?

30. What is the product of $\frac{1}{2}$ of $\frac{3}{4}$ of 16 multiplied by $5\frac{5}{7}$?

31. What is the value of $\frac{3}{4}$ of $\frac{1}{5}$ of $6\frac{2}{3}$?

32. What is the value of $\frac{7}{8}$ of $\frac{4}{5}$ of 30?

33. What is the value of $\frac{2}{5}$ of $\frac{1}{7}$ of $\frac{4}{2}$?

34. What is $9\frac{3}{10}$ times $\frac{5}{6}$? $4\frac{1}{9}$ times $\frac{7}{11}$?

35. What is $10\frac{1}{2}$ times $2\frac{3}{4}$? $2\frac{1}{3}$ times $25\frac{1}{2}$?

56.   1. If 3 pounds of raisins cost $\$\frac{6}{7}$, what will 1 pound cost?

ANALYSIS. *If 3 pounds cost $\$\frac{6}{7}$, 1 pound, which is $\frac{1}{3}$ of 3 pounds, will cost $\frac{1}{3}$ of $\$\frac{6}{7}$, or $\$\frac{2}{7}$. Therefore, &c.*

2. If 4 slates cost $\$\frac{8}{9}$, what will 1 slate cost?

3. If 5 pounds of sugar cost $\$\frac{5}{9}$, what will 1 pound ost?

4. If 3 oranges are worth $\frac{6}{7}$ of a melon, what part of the melon is 1 orange worth?

NOTE. It will be remembered that a *fraction* may be *divided* by a *whole* number either by *dividing* the *numerator* or *multiplying* the *denominator* by it. (See pages 72 and 73, notes.)

5. If 6 pounds of coffee cost $\$\frac{3}{5}$, what will 1 pound cost?

6. If 4 apples cost $\frac{5}{6}$ of a shilling, what will 1 apple cost?

7. If 5 yards of sheeting cost $\$\frac{6}{9}$, what will 1 yard cost?

8. If 4 figs cost $\frac{2}{6}$ of a dime, what will 1 fig cost?

9. What will 1 yard of linen cost, if 4 yards cost $\$\frac{1}{4}$?

10. Marcus had $\frac{3}{4}$ of a melon, which he wished to divide equally between his 2 sisters; what part must he give to each?

11. Oliver, having 12 quarts of blueberries, sold $\frac{2}{3}$ of them for $\$\frac{4}{5}$; what was that a quart?

12. If 6 persons agree to share equally $\frac{3}{4}$ of a bushel of grapes, what part of a bushel will each have?

13. If you divide $\frac{7}{8}$ of a barrel of flour among 3 poor families, what part of a barrel will you give to each?

14. How many times is 7 contained in $\frac{6}{8}$? 5 in $\frac{10}{11}$? 8 in $\frac{6}{7}$? 10 in $\frac{40}{19}$?

15. What is the quotient of $\frac{35}{49}$ divided by 5? by 7?

16. What is the quotient of $\frac{6}{7}$ divided by 3? by 4?

57. 1. At $\$\frac{3}{4}$ a yard, how many yards of silk can be bought for $6 ?

ANALYSIS. *As many yards as $\$\frac{3}{4}$, the price of 1 yard, is contained times in $6 ; $6 is equal to $\$2\frac{4}{4}$, and $\$\frac{3}{4}$ is contained in $\$2\frac{4}{4}$ 8 times. Therefore, at $\$\frac{3}{4}$ a yard, 8 yards of silk can be bought for $6.*

2. If a boy can earn $\$\frac{3}{5}$ a day, how long will it take him to earn $5 ?

3. How long will it take a man to spend $10 for cigars, if he spend $\$\frac{1}{4}$ a day ?

4. When potatoes are $\$\frac{2}{3}$ per bushel, how many bushels can be bought for $8 ?

5. At $\$\frac{7}{9}$ a pair, how many pairs of shoes can be bought for $7 ?

6. How much butter can be bought for $3, at $\$\frac{1}{6}$ a pound ?

7. How many times is $\frac{1}{3}$ contained in 4 ? in 7 ? in 8 ?

8. If the cars run $\frac{2}{5}$ of a mile a minute, how long will they be in running 25 miles ?

9. If a horse eat $\frac{3}{7}$ of a bushel of oats a day, how long will 9 bushels last him ?

10. If a man walk $\frac{4}{5}$ of a mile in $\frac{1}{8}$ of an hour, how long will it take him to walk 12 miles ?

11. How many bushels of oats, worth $\$\frac{2}{5}$ a bushel, will pay for $\frac{2}{3}$ of a barrel of flour, worth $9 a barrel ?

12. A farmer sold a grocer 1 ton of hay for $12, and received $\frac{1}{2}$ the amount in sugar at $\$\frac{1}{8}$ a pound, $\frac{1}{3}$ in money, and the remainder in molasses at $\$\frac{2}{5}$ a gallon ; how many pounds of sugar, and how many gallons of molasses, did he receive ?

13. If $\frac{7}{8}$ of a barrel of trout cost $12, what will 1 barrel cost ?

14. If $\frac{5}{8}$ of a ton of hay cost $7, what will 1 ton cost ?

15. When potatoes are worth $\frac{4}{9}$ a bushel, and corn $\frac{5}{8}$ a bushel, how many bushels of potatoes are equal in value to 16 bushels of corn?

16. How many yards of ribbon, at $\frac{5}{7}$ of a shilling a yard, can be bought for 7 shillings?

17. If 1 man consume $\frac{3}{4}$ of a pound of meat in a day, how many men would 6 pounds supply?

18. If $\frac{6}{7}$ of a hogshead of molasses cost $36, what will one hogshead cost?

19. If $\frac{3}{7}$ of an acre of land sell for $21, what will an acre sell for at the same rate?

20. How many pounds of tea, worth $\frac{7}{12}$ a pound, must be given for 9 bushels of apples, worth $\frac{4}{9}$ a bushel?

21. How many times is $\frac{2}{7}$ contained in 5? in 7? in 9? in 11? in 15?

22. How many times is $\frac{5}{9}$ contained in 12? in 18? in 20? in 15?

23. How many times is $\frac{1}{6}$ contained in $\frac{3}{8}$? in $\frac{12}{13}$? in $\frac{24}{25}$? in $\frac{4}{5}$?

24. How many times is $\frac{1}{3}$ contained in $\frac{3}{4}$ of 16? in $\frac{5}{9}$ of 27?

25. How is a whole number divided by a fraction?

---

58. 1. At $2 a bushel, how many bushels of wheat can be bought for 11\frac{1}{3}$?

ANALYSIS. *As many bushels as $2, the price of 1 bushel, is contained times in 11\frac{1}{3}$. 11$\frac{1}{3}$ are equal to $\frac{34}{3}$, and 2 is contained in $\frac{34}{3}$, $\frac{17}{3}$, or 5$\frac{2}{3}$ times. Therefore, &c.*

Or, 2 is contained in 11$\frac{1}{3}$, 5 times, and 1$\frac{1}{3}$ or $\frac{4}{3}$ over; and 2 is contained in $\frac{4}{3}$, $\frac{2}{3}$ times, which added to 5 makes 5$\frac{2}{3}$ times. Therefore, &c.

2. If 6 pounds of coffee cost 1\frac{5}{8}$, what is the cost of 1 pound?

3. If a man walk $18\frac{2}{3}$ miles in 4 hours, how many miles does he walk in 1 hour?

4. How many times will $16\frac{3}{4}$ gallons of cider fill a vessel that holds 3 gallons?

5. How many oranges, at 3 cents apiece, can be bought for $\frac{4}{5}$ of $\frac{1}{3}$ of 60 cents?

6. At $4 a yard, how many yards of cloth can be bought for $$21\frac{5}{7}$?

7. If a turkey cost 7 shillings, how many turkeys can be bought for $38\frac{1}{2}$ shillings?

8. At 5 shillings a gallon, how many gallons of molasses can be bought for $24\frac{3}{8}$ shillings?

9. If a day laborer earn $$8\frac{3}{4}$ in 10 days, how much does he earn in 1 day?

10. If a locomotive run $4\frac{2}{3}$ miles in 6 minutes, how far does she run in 1 minute?

11. If 12 bushels of oats cost $$4\frac{1}{2}$, what part of a dollar will 1 bushel cost?

12. If 7 pounds of coffee cost $8\frac{1}{2}$ dimes, what will 1 pound cost?

13. Divide $8\frac{1}{3}$ by 5; $10\frac{2}{7}$ by 7; $15\frac{1}{6}$ by 15.

14. Divide $9\frac{4}{5}$ by 7; $18\frac{1}{2}$ by 12; $20\frac{1}{4}$ by $\frac{1}{2}$ of 16.

15. Divide $\frac{3}{4}$ of 21 by $\frac{2}{5}$ of 10. $\frac{7}{8}$ of 29 by $\frac{1}{9}$ of 63.

---

59. 1. At $$\frac{2}{5}$ a pound, how many pounds of *tea* can be bought for $$\frac{3}{4}$?

ANALYSIS. *As many pounds as* $$\frac{2}{5}$, *the price of* 1 *pound, is contained times in* $$\frac{3}{4}$. $\frac{2}{5}$ *equal* $\frac{8}{20}$, $\frac{3}{4}$ *equal* $\frac{15}{20}$, *and* 8 *twentieths are contained in* 15 *twentieths* $1\frac{7}{8}$ *times. Therefore, at* $$\frac{2}{5}$ *a pound,* $1\frac{7}{8}$ *pounds can be bought for* $$\frac{3}{4}$.

Or thus: $\frac{1}{5}$ *is contained in* 1, 5 *times, and in* $\frac{3}{4}$ *of* 1 *it is contained* $\frac{3}{4}$ *of* 5 *times, or* $\frac{15}{4}$ *times;* $\frac{2}{5}$ *is contained in* $\frac{3}{4}$, $\frac{1}{2}$ *as many times, and* $\frac{1}{2}$ *of* $\frac{15}{4}$ *is* $\frac{15}{8}$, *or* $1\frac{7}{8}$.

2. How many pounds of honey, at $\$\frac{1}{4}$ a pound, can be bought for $\$\frac{7}{8}$?

3. In $\frac{9}{6}$ of an acre of land, how many building lots of $\frac{3}{10}$ of an acre each ?

4. If a horse eat $\frac{3}{8}$ of a bushel of oats in a day in how many days will he eat $\frac{9}{10}$ of a bushel ?

5. At $\frac{3}{4}$ of a cent apiece, how many slate pencils can be bought for $\frac{8}{3}$ of a cent ?

6. If a piece of ribbon $\frac{8}{9}$ of a yard long be cut into pieces $\frac{1}{6}$ of a yard in length, how many pieces will there be ?

7. A man, owning $\frac{5}{8}$ of a coal mine, divided his share equally among his sons, giving them $\frac{5}{16}$ each; how many sons had he ?

8. Among how many children can you divide $\frac{3}{4}$ of $1\frac{2}{3}$ melons, if you give $\frac{1}{2}$ of $\frac{1}{4}$ of a melon to each ?

9. At $\$\frac{7}{8}$ a yard, how many yards of silk can be bought for $\$\frac{5}{3}$?

10. At $\frac{4}{5}$ of $\frac{1}{3}$ of a dollar a yard, how many yards of ribbon can be bought for $\$\frac{7}{10}$?

11. At $\$\frac{7}{10}$ a pint, how much wine can be bought for $\$\frac{1}{2}$?

12. When peaches are worth $\$\frac{5}{6}$ a bushel, how many can be bought for $\$\frac{3}{4}$?

13. If $\frac{2}{3}$ of a yard of silk cost $\$\frac{3}{4}$, what will 1 yard cost ?

ANALYSIS. *It will cost 3 times $\frac{1}{2}$ of $\$\frac{3}{4}$, or $\frac{3}{2}$ of $\$\frac{3}{4}$. $\frac{1}{2}$ of $\frac{3}{4}$ is $\frac{3}{8}$, and 3 times $\frac{3}{8}$ are $\frac{9}{8}$, or $\$1\frac{1}{8}$. Therefore, if $\frac{2}{3}$ of a yard of silk cost $\$\frac{3}{4}$, 1 yard will cost $\$1\frac{1}{8}$.*

14. What will 1 dozen eggs cost, if $\frac{5}{6}$ of a dozen cost $\frac{2}{3}$ of a dime ?

15. If $\frac{5}{8}$ of a bushel of corn are worth $\frac{10}{4}$ of a bushel of rye, how many bushels of corn is 1 bushel of rye worth ?

16. Horace had $\$\frac{5}{8}$, which was $\frac{5}{9}$ of what he paid for a cap; what was the cost of his cap ?

59.]   INTELLECTUAL ARITHMETIC.   93

17. If $\frac{2}{3}$ of a yard of cloth cost $\$\frac{8}{10}$, what will 1 yard cost?

18. James bought $\frac{2}{5}$ of a pineapple, which was $\frac{2}{3}$ of what Luther bought; what part of a pineapple did Luther buy?

19. If $\frac{2}{7}$ of a drum of figs cost $\$\frac{5}{8}$, what will 1 drum cost?

20. How many times can a bottle holding $\frac{1}{4}$ of $\frac{2}{3}$ of a gallon be filled from a demijohn containing $\frac{3}{4}$ of $1\frac{2}{3}$ gallons?

21. Divide $\frac{7}{8}$ by $\frac{2}{5}$; $\frac{9}{10}$ by $\frac{2}{3}$.

22. Divide $\frac{12}{13}$ by $\frac{4}{7}$; $\frac{9}{11}$ by $\frac{3}{2}$.

23. Divide $\frac{5}{8}$ by $\frac{1}{6}$; $\frac{8}{9}$ by $\frac{5}{8}$.

24. Divide $\frac{1}{2}$ of $\frac{5}{9}$ by $\frac{3}{4}$; $\frac{2}{3}$ of $\frac{4}{5}$ by $\frac{1}{4}$ of $\frac{2}{7}$.

25. Divide $\frac{13}{11}$ by $\frac{1}{2}$ of $\frac{2}{3}$; $\frac{9}{20}$ by $\frac{4}{9}$.

26. Divide $\frac{30}{35}$ by $\frac{3}{10}$; $\frac{7}{36}$ by $\frac{1}{12}$.

27. How many times are $\frac{2}{7}$ contained in $\frac{4}{14}$?

28. How many times are $\frac{3}{8}$ contained in $\frac{3}{16}$?

29. How many times are $\frac{3}{4}$ contained in $\frac{5}{9}$?

30. How many times are $\frac{2}{3}$ contained in $\frac{11}{16}$?

31. How many times are $\frac{6}{7}$ contained in $\frac{3}{5}$?

32. How many times are $\frac{2}{3}$ of $\frac{4}{5}$ contained in $\frac{11}{12}$?

33. How many times are $\frac{7}{4}$ contained in $\frac{2}{3}$ of $1\frac{1}{4}$?

34. How many times are $\frac{1}{5}$ of $\frac{3}{8}$ contained in $\frac{1}{2}$ of $\frac{9}{4}$?

35. $\frac{4}{9}$ are $\frac{3}{4}$ of what number?

ANALYSIS. $\frac{4}{9}$ *are* $\frac{3}{4}$ *of* 4 *times* $\frac{1}{3}$ *of* $\frac{4}{9}$; $\frac{1}{3}$ *of* $\frac{4}{9}$ *are* $\frac{4}{27}$ *and* 4 *times* $\frac{4}{27}$ *are* $\frac{16}{27}$. *Therefore,* $\frac{4}{9}$ *are* $\frac{3}{4}$ *of* $\frac{16}{27}$.

36. $\frac{3}{7}$ are $\frac{2}{3}$ of what number?

37. $\frac{8}{9}$ are $\frac{5}{8}$ of what number?

38. $\frac{2}{15}$ are $\frac{2}{7}$ of what number?

39. $\frac{3}{4}$ are $\frac{6}{7}$ of what number?

40. $\frac{7}{12}$ are $\frac{1}{2}$ of what number?

60.   1. At $1\frac{5}{6}$ dollars a yard, how many yards of cloth can be bought for $11?

ANALYSIS. *As many yards as* $1\frac{5}{6}$, *the price of* 1 *yard, is contained times in* $11. $1\frac{5}{6}$ *are* $\frac{11}{6}$; $11 *are* $\frac{66}{6}$, *and* $\frac{11}{6}$ *is contained in* $\frac{66}{6}$, 6 *times. Therefore, at* $1\frac{5}{6}$ *a yard,* 6 *yards of cloth can be bought for* $11.

2. If a turkey cost $1\frac{2}{8}$, how many can be bought for $9?

3. A grocer paid $4\frac{3}{5}$ for some onions, at the rate of $\frac{2}{3}$ a bushel; how many did he buy?

4. How many times will $4\frac{3}{4}$ gallons of camphene fill a vessel that holds $\frac{1}{2}$ of $\frac{2}{3}$ of 1 gallon?

5. If $4\frac{3}{4}$ yards of velvet ribbon cost $\frac{7}{8}$, what will 1 yard cost?

6. If $3\frac{1}{2}$ dozen of eggs cost $\frac{7}{16}$, what is the cost of 1 dozen?

7. How many yards of flannel worth $\frac{2}{3}$ a yard can be bought for 6 turkeys worth $\frac{8}{8}$ apiece?

8. If 1 man can do a piece of work in $6\frac{7}{8}$ days, in what time can 4 men do the same?

9. If a man chop $1\frac{1}{6}$ cords of wood in a day, how long will it take him to chop $10\frac{1}{2}$ cords?

NOTE. Reduce the mixed numbers to improper fractions, and then divide the same as you divide one fraction by another.

10. If $4\frac{1}{3}$ baskets of peaches are worth $3\frac{3}{4}$, what is 1 basket worth?

11. If $5\frac{1}{3}$ bushels of apples cost $1\frac{7}{9}$, what is the cost of 1 bushel?

12. If a man spend $1\frac{5}{6}$ a month for tobacco, in what time will he spend $10\frac{1}{3}$ for the same purpose?

13. At $4\frac{1}{2}$ shillings a gallon, how many gallons of molasses can be bought for $9\frac{3}{4}$ shillings?

14. If a stage run $24\frac{3}{4}$ miles in $3\frac{1}{2}$ hours, how far does it run in 1 hour?

15. Mr. B. distributed $16\frac{1}{2}$ bushels of corn equally

among some poor persons, giving them $1\frac{1}{2}$ bushels each ; among how many persons did he divide it ?

16. Bought $\frac{1}{3}$ of $7\frac{1}{2}$ cords of wood for $\frac{1}{4}$ of $32 ; what did 1 cord cost ?

17. A father divided $113\frac{1}{3}$ acres of land among his 3 sons ; to the first he gave $\frac{2}{5}$ of it, and the remainder he divided equally between the other 2 ; how many acres did each receive ?

18. Divide $9\frac{1}{4}$ by 6 ; $10\frac{1}{3}$ by 7 ; $12\frac{2}{5}$ by 31.

19. Divide $10\frac{1}{8}$ by $\frac{3}{4}$; $14\frac{1}{2}$ by $\frac{2}{3}$; $20\frac{1}{4}$ by $\frac{3}{4}$.

20. Divide $7\frac{1}{3}$ by $3\frac{2}{5}$; $15\frac{1}{5}$ by $2\frac{4}{5}$; $8\frac{6}{8}$ by $5\frac{1}{2}$.

21. Divide $16\frac{1}{4}$ by $3\frac{1}{4}$; $20\frac{1}{2}$ by $1\frac{7}{10}$; $11\frac{1}{5}$ by $4\frac{2}{3}$

22.. Divide $\frac{3}{4}$ of $\frac{1}{2}$ of 14 by $\frac{2}{5}$ of $3\frac{1}{2}$.

23. $\frac{7}{9}$ are how many times   6 ?

24. $\frac{8}{11}$ are how many times   4 ?

25. $\frac{9}{16}$ are how many times   15 ?

26. $\frac{10}{3}$ are how many times $6\frac{1}{4}$?

27.   12 are how many times $\frac{3}{8}$?

28.   16 are how many times $\frac{4}{9}$?

29.   25 are how many times $\frac{3}{8}$?

30.   14 are how many times $\frac{7}{10}$?

31. $14\frac{2}{3}$ are how many times $\frac{4}{6}$?

32. $6\frac{4}{5}$ are how many times $\frac{4}{3}$?

33. $21\frac{1}{4}$ are how many times   5 ?

34. $32\frac{2}{3}$ are how many times   7 ?

35. $17\frac{2}{6}$ are how many times   8 ?

36.   15 are how many times $7\frac{1}{2}$?

37. $18\frac{2}{3}$ are how many times $2\frac{1}{4}$?

38. $22\frac{1}{2}$ are how many times $3\frac{3}{4}$?

39. $4\frac{9}{10}$ are how many times $6\frac{2}{5}$?

40. $7\frac{2}{9}$ are how many times $4\frac{1}{6}$?

41. $8\frac{3}{4}$ are how many times $3\frac{2}{3}$?

61. 1. What is $\frac{1}{4}$ of 3 ?

ANALYSIS. *That number which, taken 4 times, will make 3. Since 1 fourth of 1 is $\frac{1}{4}$, 1 fourth of 3 is 3 times $\frac{1}{4}$ of 1, or $\frac{3}{4}$ of 1. Therefore $\frac{1}{4}$ of 3 is $\frac{3}{4}$ of 1, or $\frac{3}{4}$.*

2. What is $\frac{1}{2}$ of 3 ? of 4 ? of 6 ? of 7 ?
3. What is $\frac{1}{5}$ of 7 ? of 3 ? of 9 ? of 15 ?
4. What is $\frac{1}{3}$ of 2 ? of 4 ? of 5 ? of 11 ?
5. What is $\frac{1}{6}$ of 3 ? of 5 ? of 7 ? of 13 ?
6. What is $\frac{1}{4}$ of 2 ? of 3 ? of 5 ? of 7 ?
7. What is $\frac{1}{8}$ of 3 ? of 5 ? of 9 ? of 14 ?
8. What is $\frac{1}{7}$ of 4 ? of 6 ? of 12 ? of 18 ?
9. What is $\frac{1}{9}$ of 5 ? of 3 ? of 20 ? of 30 ?
10. What is $\frac{1}{10}$ of 7 ? of 9 ? of 16 ? of 47 ?
11. What is $\frac{1}{15}$ of 4 ? of 7 ? of 11 ? of 63 ?
12. What is $\frac{1}{12}$ of 2 ? of 7 ? of 11 ? of 34 ? of 75 ?
13. What is $\frac{1}{20}$ of 13 ? of 9 ? of 17 ? of 50 ? of 91 ?
14. If 5 bushels of wheat cost $9, what will 1 bushel cost ?

ANALYSIS. *If 5 bushels cost $9, 1 bushel, which is $\frac{1}{5}$ of 5 bushels, will cost $\frac{1}{5}$ of $9 ; $\frac{1}{5}$ of $9 is 1\frac{4}{5}$. Therefore, if 5 bushels cost $9, 1 bushel will cost 1\frac{4}{5}$.*

15. If 6 turkeys are worth $5, what are they worth apiece ?
16. If you divide 6 oranges equally among 7 boys, what part of an orange will each receive ?
17. If a man travel 29 miles in 9 hours, how far does he travel in 1 hour ?
18. If 1 man can build a barn in 20 days, in what time can 3 men build it ?
19. If a horse eat 5 bushels of oats in 8 days, what part of a bushel does he eat in 1 day ?
20. What will 1 hat cost, if 4 hats cost $17 ?

62.   1. What are $\frac{3}{4}$ of 3 ?

ANALYSIS. $\frac{3}{4}$ *of* 3 *are* 3 *times* $\frac{1}{4}$ *of* 3 ; $\frac{1}{4}$ *of* 3 *is* $\frac{3}{4}$ *of* 1, *and* 3 *times* $\frac{3}{4}$ *are* $\frac{9}{4}$ *or* $2\frac{1}{4}$. *Therefore,* $\frac{3}{4}$ *of* 3 *are* $2\frac{1}{4}$.

  2. What are $\frac{2}{3}$ of   5 ? of   4 ? of   7 ?
  3. What are $\frac{5}{6}$ of   4 ? of   5 ? of 8 ?
  4. What are $\frac{3}{5}$ of   2 ? of   3 ? of   9 ?
  5. What are $\frac{4}{7}$ of   3 ? of   5 ? of 10 ? of 12 ?
  6. What are $\frac{3}{10}$ of   4 ? of   7 ? of 15 ? of 18 ?
  7. What are $\frac{5}{8}$ of   2 ? of   3 ? of 14 ? of 20 ?
  8. What are $\frac{2}{9}$ of   5 ? of   8 ? of 19 ? of 28 ?
  9. What are $\frac{5}{11}$ of   7 ? of 13 ? of 21 ? of 30 ?
10. What are $\frac{6}{7}$ of   2 ? of   6 ? of 15 ? of 24 ?
11. What are $\frac{5}{12}$ of   7 ? of 36 ? of 50 ? of 63 ?
12. What are $\frac{4}{15}$ of 35 ? of 60 ? of 77 ? of 91 ?
13. What are $\frac{7}{20}$ of 10 ? of 15 ? of 120 ? of 150 ?
14. If 4 cords of wood cost $14, what will 5 cords cost ?

ANALYSIS. *If* 4 *cords of wood cost* $14, 5 *cords will cost* 5 *times* $\frac{1}{4}$ *of* $14. $\frac{1}{4}$ *of* $14 *is* $3\frac{1}{2}$, *and* 5 *times* $3\frac{1}{2}$ *are* $17\frac{1}{2}$. *Therefore* 5 *cords of wood will cost* $17\frac{1}{2}$.

15. If 3 bushels of quinces cost $7, what will 2 bushels cost ?
16. If 9 bushels of apples cost $4, what will 7 bushels cost ?
17. At 6 cents for 2 oranges, how many oranges could you buy for 21 cents ?
18. If 4 men can do a piece of work in 15 days, in what time can 6 men do the same ?
19. If a quantity of provision will last 5 men 9 days, how long would the same last 11 men ?

63. 1. If 1 pound of butter cost 19 cents, what will $\frac{5}{6}$ of a pound cost?

2. A barrel of beer sold for $8; what was $\frac{2}{8}$ of it worth?

3. Sold a cow for $18, which was only $\frac{7}{8}$ of her real value; what was her real value?

4. Bought a carriage for $65, and afterwards sold it for $\frac{9}{8}$ of what it cost me; how much did I gain?

5. A farmer, having 80 sheep, sold $\frac{7}{10}$ of them; how many had he left?

6. If I give 4 pounds of butter, worth $12\frac{1}{2}$ cents a pound, for 8 pounds of sugar, what is the sugar worth a pound?

7. After paying $\frac{3}{5}$ of my money for a piece of land, I had $48 left; how much money had I at first?

8. A man bought a watch and chain for $50, which was $\frac{7}{6}$ of what the watch alone cost; what was the cost of each?

9. If a man can cut 9 cords of wood in $\frac{4}{5}$ of a week, how many cords can he cut in 4 weeks?

10. A man paid $35 for a book-case, $\frac{4}{7}$ of the cost of his book-case was $\frac{4}{5}$ of what he paid for a bureau, and $\frac{3}{4}$ the cost of the bureau was $\frac{5}{4}$ of what he paid for a table; what did he pay for the bureau, and for the table?

11. If 4 quarts of chestnuts cost 37 cents, what will 1 bushel cost?

12. If a man can walk 7 miles in 2 hours, how far can he walk in 3 days, by walking 10 hours a day?

13. If $\frac{5}{7}$ of a barrel of flour is worth $8, what are 12 barrels worth?

14. If 3 pecks of grass-seed cost 14 shillings, what will 4 quarts cost?

15. If 3 yards of silk cost $\$19\frac{1}{2}$, what will 7 yards cost?

16. If a man earn $\$32\frac{1}{3}$ in 4 weeks, how much will he earn in 2 weeks?

17. If \$9 will buy $4\frac{2}{3}$ yards of cloth, how much will \$1 buy?

18. A man, having $56\frac{3}{4}$ acres of land, sold $\frac{2}{3}$ of it; how many acres did he sell?

19. If 9 horses eat $5\frac{5}{8}$ bushels of oats in a day, how many bushels will 4 horses eat in the same time?

20. If 3 yards of flannel cost $\$\frac{5}{6}$, what will 8 yards cost?

21. If 10 bushels of wheat are worth $22\frac{1}{2}$ bushels of corn, how many bushels of corn are 3 bushels of wheat worth?

22. If 14 acres of meadow land produce $32\frac{2}{3}$ tons of hay, how many tons will 5 acres of the same land produce?

23. A cistern is filled by 3 pipes in $6\frac{3}{4}$ hours; how many pipes of the same size will be required to fill it in $\frac{1}{4}$ of an hour?

24. A boy sold 5 quarts of strawberries at the rate of 3 quarts for 13 cents; how much did he receive for the whole?

25. A tailor bought 3 pieces of cassimere, each piece containing $6\frac{2}{3}$ yards, for $\$48\frac{4}{7}$; how much did it cost a piece, and how much a yard?

26. If a pole 8 feet long cast a shadow 6 feet, how long is a pole that casts a shadow $12\frac{1}{2}$ feet at the same time?

27. How much less than \$17 will 9 yards of satin cost, if 2 yards cost $\$3\frac{1}{4}$?

28. If 3 yards of velvet cost $\$5\frac{1}{4}$, how much more than \$9 will 6 yards of it cost?

29. If a horse travel $40\frac{2}{7}$ miles in 6 hours, how far will he travel in 4 hours?

64. 1. If 5 pounds of chalk cost $28\frac{1}{3}$ cents, what will $\frac{3}{4}$ of a pound cost?

2. If 3 pairs of socks cost $\$\frac{9}{10}$, how many pairs can be bought for $\$2\frac{7}{10}$?

3. Lucas is $\frac{3}{7}$ as old as his father, who is 60 years of age; what is Lucas's age?

4. If $\frac{1}{4}$ of a box of raisins cost $\$2\frac{1}{12}$, what will $\frac{5}{6}$ of a box cost?

5. A boy sold some peaches for $6\frac{3}{4}$ cents, at the rate of 3 for $4\frac{1}{2}$ cents; how many did he sell?

6. If 7 bushels of oats cost $\$1\frac{5}{9}$, what will $12\frac{3}{4}$ bushels cost?

7. If $2\frac{5}{8}$ yards of shalloon cost $\$4\frac{1}{5}$, what will 5 yards cost?

8. Bought $4\frac{1}{2}$ barrels of cider at $\$3\frac{4}{5}$ a barrel, and paid in wood at \$3 a cord; how many cords of wood paid for the cider?

9. John has $\$5\frac{1}{7}$, and Gilbert has $1\frac{2}{5}$ times as much; how much has Gilbert?

10. Three men incur an expense of $\$27\frac{2}{3}$; how much more than $\$7\frac{1}{2}$ must each pay?

11. A man, being asked his age, said that, were he 3 times as old, $\frac{1}{12}$ of his age would be 8 years; how old was he?

12. If a pound of tea is worth $3\frac{1}{3}$ times as much as a pound of coffee, what will $6\frac{4}{5}$ pounds of coffee cost, when tea is worth 50 cents a pound?

13. If $2\frac{2}{3}$ pounds of cheese cost 20 cents, what will 12 pounds cost?

14. If $3\frac{1}{4}$ barrels of apples cost $\$5\frac{1}{5}$, what will $\frac{1}{2}$ barrel cost?

15. A stone mason worked $11\frac{2}{3}$ days, and after paying his board and other expenses with $\frac{3}{7}$ of his earnings, had \$20 left; how much did he receive a day?

16. If 7 bushels of potatoes cost $\$3\frac{1}{2}$, how many bushels can be bought for $\$14\frac{1}{2}$?

17. If $\frac{1}{3}$ of a quart of brandy cost $\$\frac{3}{7}$, how many gallons will $\$12\frac{6}{7}$ buy?

18. How many yards of silk can be bought for 30 shillings, if 3 shillings be paid for $\frac{3}{5}$ of a yard?

19. If $\frac{4}{5}$ of a shilling will buy $\frac{4}{7}$ of a pound of butter, how many pounds will 7 shillings buy?

20. How many gallons of molasses can be bought for $\$3\frac{1}{2}$, if $\frac{1}{5}$ of a gallon cost $\$\frac{1}{7}$?

21. How many oats can be bought for 10 shillings, if 9 bushels cost 24 shillings?

22. If 5 dozen of eggs cost $4\frac{2}{7}$ shillings, how many dozen can be bought for 7 shillings?

23. If 8 yards of velvet ribbon cost $\$1\frac{7}{9}$, how many yards can be bought for $\$3\frac{1}{2}$?

24. How many pints of alcohol will 3 shillings buy, if $\frac{1}{6}$ of a pint cost $\frac{1}{4}$ of a shilling?

25. If a man eat $1\frac{2}{3}$ pounds of bread in a day, how many days will $22\frac{1}{3}$ pounds last him?

26. How many pounds of sugar worth 10 cents a pound can be had for $6\frac{2}{3}$ pounds of cheese worth $7\frac{1}{2}$ cents a pound?

27. If a horse consume $8\frac{1}{4}$ bushels of oats in 3 weeks, how many bushels would he consume in 5 weeks?

28. A man gave $6\frac{2}{3}$ pounds of butter at 12 cents a pound for $\frac{4}{5}$ of a gallon of oil; what was the oil worth a gallon?

29. When 4 pounds of tea can be bought for $\$2\frac{2}{5}$, how much can be bought for $\$\frac{9}{10}$?

30. A man, having $10, gave $\frac{2}{3}$ of his money for clover seed at $\$3\frac{1}{3}$ a bushel; how much did he buy?

31. If $\frac{5}{9}$ of a bushel of rye cost $\$\frac{1}{2}$, how many bushels can be bought for $7?

65. 1. If $\frac{1}{2}$ a yard of cloth cost $\$\frac{2}{5}$, what will $\frac{1}{8}$ of a yard cost?

2. If $\frac{3}{4}$ of 2 pounds of tea cost $\$1\frac{1}{2}$, what will $\frac{4}{6}$ of 1 pound cost?

3. What will $\frac{4}{9}$ of a barrel of apples cost, if $\frac{2}{7}$ of a barrel cost $\$\frac{2}{3}$?

4. If $\frac{7}{8}$ of a pound of butter is worth $\frac{7}{3}$ of a pound of fish, how many pounds of fish are $1\frac{1}{4}$ pounds of butter worth?

5. What will be the cost of 6 barrels of flour at the rate of $\$2\frac{3}{5}$ for every $\frac{2}{5}$ of a barrel?

6. At $\$\frac{1}{6}$ a quart, what part of a bushel of clover seed can be bought for $\$3\frac{1}{3}$?

7. Since I was 25 years old, $\frac{3}{8}$ of my entire age has passed; what is my age?

8. A man, engaging in play, lost $\frac{1}{3}$ of his money, after which he gained $\$75$, when he found that he had $\$375$; how much money did he lose?

9. If 4 horses consume $2\frac{2}{3}$ bushels of oats in $2\frac{1}{2}$ days, how many bushels will 6 horses consume in the same time?

10. If $\frac{3}{5}$ of a bushel of barley be given for $\frac{3}{4}$ of a bushel of corn worth $\$\frac{2}{3}$ a bushel, what is the barley worth a bushel?

11. A person having a drove of turkeys, after selling 35, found that he had $\frac{4}{9}$ of his drove left; how many turkeys in his drove at first?

12. What number is that to which if $\frac{5}{6}$ of itself be added, the number will be 55?

13. What number added to 3 times $\frac{2}{5}$ of 27 will make the number 40?

14. If 24 is $\frac{3}{5}$ of some number, what is $\frac{4}{7}$ of the same number?

15. What number taken from $2\frac{1}{2}$ times $12\frac{4}{5}$ will leave $20\frac{3}{4}$?

16. If $40 exceed by $10, $\frac{1}{2}$ of $\frac{3}{4}$ of what I gained in the sale of a house and lot, how much did I gain?

17. If $\frac{2}{5}$ of 4 tons of coal cost 5\frac{1}{8}$, what will $\frac{3}{4}$ of 2 tons cost?

18. A young lady, being asked her age, replied that 5 times $\frac{1}{3}$ of 30 years was 4$\frac{1}{4}$ years more than 3 times her age; what was her age?

19. In an orchard, $\frac{1}{2}$ the trees bear apples, $\frac{1}{6}$ bear peaches, $\frac{1}{12}$ bear pears and 15 trees bear plums; how many trees in the orchard, and how many of each kind?

20. How many yards of cloth that is $\frac{4}{5}$ of a yard wide are equal to 12 yards $\frac{3}{4}$ of a yard wide?

21. A, B, and C can do a piece of work in 5 days; B and C can do it in 8 days; in what time can A do it alone?

22. A can build a piece of wall in 3 days, and B can build it in 4 days; in what time can both build it together?

23. If $\frac{2}{3}$ the value of a carriage is equal to $\frac{3}{4}$ the value of a horse, and the difference in their values is $25, what is the value of each?

24. A tailor paid $73, which was $\frac{7}{12}$ of all the money he had, for cloth, at the rate of $3 a yard; how many yards could he have purchased with all his money, at the same rate?

25. A father divided a piece of land among his 3 sons; to the first he gave 10$\frac{1}{2}$ acres, to the second $\frac{2}{3}$ of the whole, and to the. third as much as to the other two; how many acres had each?

26. A farmer bought 2 cows for $56, paying $\frac{3}{4}$ as much for one as for the other; how much did each cost him?

27. A and B can do a piece of work in 14 days; A can do $\frac{3}{4}$ as much as B; in how many days can each do it?

66.   1. 16 is $\frac{4}{5}$ of what number?

ANALYSIS.   16 *is* $\frac{4}{5}$ *of* 5 *times* $\frac{1}{4}$ *of* 16; $\frac{1}{4}$ *of* 16 *is* 4, *and* 5 *times* 4 *are* 20.   *Therefore,* 16 *is* $\frac{4}{5}$ *of* 20.

Or thus: *Since* 16 *is* $\frac{4}{5}$ *of some number,* $\frac{1}{5}$ *of the number, which is* $\frac{1}{4}$ *of* $\frac{4}{5}$, *is* $\frac{1}{4}$ *of* 16, *or* 4; *and* 4 *is* $\frac{1}{5}$ *of* 5 *times* 4, *or* 20.   *Therefore, &c.*

   2. 42 is $\frac{6}{7}$ of what number?
   3. 25 is $\frac{5}{3}$ of what number?
   4. 16 is $\frac{4}{7}$ of what number?
   5. 32 is $\frac{8}{9}$ of what number?
   6. 60 is $\frac{6}{11}$ of what number?
   7. 14 is $\frac{7}{5}$ of what number?
   8. 48 is $\frac{4}{7}$ of what number?
   9. 75 is $\frac{3}{4}$ of what number?
  10. 84 is $\frac{12}{20}$ of what number?
  11. 55 is $\frac{11}{28}$ of what number?
  12. 64 is $\frac{8}{15}$ of what number?
  13. 13 is $\frac{3}{2}$ of what number?
  14. 18 is $\frac{5}{6}$ of what number?
  15. 28 is $\frac{3}{8}$ of what number?
  16. 40 is $\frac{6}{7}$ of what number?
  17. 54 is $\frac{3}{10}$ of what number?
  18. 10 is $\frac{3}{15}$ of what number?
  19. $12\frac{1}{2}$ is $\frac{1}{4}$ of what number?
  20. $15\frac{3}{4}$ is $\frac{9}{7}$ of what number?
  21. $19\frac{3}{5}$ is $\frac{7}{10}$ of what number?
  22. $24\frac{1}{4}$ is $\frac{9}{12}$ of what number?
  23. $16\frac{1}{5}$ is $\frac{4}{7}$ of what number?
  24. $\frac{7}{8}$ is $\frac{2}{3}$ of what number?
  25. $\frac{4}{5}$ is $\frac{5}{6}$ of what number?
  26. $\frac{9}{10}$ is $\frac{3}{4}$ of what number? -

67.   1.   24 is $\frac{4}{5}$ of how many times 10 ? *

ANALYSIS.   24 *is* $\frac{4}{5}$ *of as many times* 10 *as* 10 *is contained times in* 5 *times* $\frac{1}{4}$ *of* 24 ; $\frac{1}{4}$ *of* 24 *is* 6, *and* 5 *times* 6 *is* 30 ; 10 *is contained in* 30, 3 *times.   Therefore* 24 *is* $\frac{4}{5}$ *of* 3 *times* 10.

2. 18 is $\frac{3}{5}$ of how many times 6 ?

3. 25 is $\frac{5}{9}$ of how many times 15 ?

4. 36 is $\frac{9}{8}$ of how many times 4 ?

5. 28 is $\frac{7}{16}$ of how many times 8 ?

6. 40 is $\frac{5}{12}$ of how many times 16 ?

7. 75 is $\frac{3}{4}$ of how many times 20 ?

8. 64 is $\frac{8}{9}$ of how many times 24 ?

9. 48 is $\frac{16}{28}$ of how many times $\frac{1}{3}$ of 30 ?

10. 35 .is $\frac{7}{4}$ of how many times $\frac{1}{7}$ of 28 ?

11. 42 is $\frac{6}{11}$ of how many times $\frac{1}{9}$ of 63 ?

12. 84 is $\frac{12}{7}$ of how many times $\frac{1}{5}$ of 35 ?

13. 27 is $\frac{9}{16}$ of how many times $\frac{1}{6}$ of 72 ?

14. 36 is $\frac{4}{2}$ of how many times $\frac{1}{3}$ of 21 ?

15. $14\frac{2}{3}$ is $\frac{4}{5}$ of how many times $\frac{1}{4}$ of 20 ?

16. $16\frac{4}{5}$ is $\frac{7}{3}$ of how many times $\frac{1}{9}$ of 54 ?

17. $12\frac{6}{7}$ is $\frac{9}{10}$ of how many times $\frac{1}{2}$ of 40 ?

18. $\frac{3}{5}$ is $\frac{4}{7}$ of how many times $\frac{1}{2}$ of $\frac{1}{3}$?

19. $\frac{1}{3}$ of $\frac{3}{4}$ is $\frac{2}{3}$ of how many times $\frac{3}{5}$ of 15 ?

20.   James gave 56 cents for a pair of skates, which was $\frac{4}{5}$ of what he gave for his sled ; what did his sled cost him ?

21.   A farmer paid $23\frac{1}{3}$ for a cow, which was $\frac{1}{4}$ of what he received for a horse ; what was the difference in the price of the cow and the horse ?

22.   A man sold $4\frac{1}{2}$ cords of wood at $2\frac{1}{2}$ a cord, which was $\frac{3}{4}$ of what he received for a ton of hay ; how much did he receive for the hay ?

* Please turn to **67** in the Appendix, page 170.

23. Paid $\$\frac{7}{8}$ for a cravat, which was $\frac{2}{7}$ of what I paid for a vest; what was the cost of the vest?

24. A gentleman bought a sleigh for $50, which was $\frac{2}{3}$ of 3 times what he paid for a harness; what did the harness cost him?

25. A lady bought a fur cape for $90, which was $\frac{10}{3}$ of what she paid for 12 yards of silk; what was the cost of the silk a yard?

26. A merchant sold 5 barrels of flour for $\$32\frac{1}{2}$, which was $\frac{5}{8}$ of what he received for all he had left, at $4 a barrel; how many barrels in all did he sell?

---

68. 1. $\frac{4}{5}$ of 20 is how many thirds of 24?

ANALYSIS. *$\frac{4}{5}$ of 20 is as many thirds of 24 as $\frac{1}{3}$ of 24 is contained times in 4 times $\frac{1}{5}$ of 20. $\frac{1}{5}$ of 20 is 4, and 4 times 4 is 16; 8 is contained in 16, 2 times. Therefore, $\frac{4}{5}$ of 20 is $\frac{2}{3}$ of 24.*

2. $\frac{7}{8}$ of 56 is how many fourths of 28?
3. $\frac{3}{8}$ of 64 is how many fifths of 60?
4. $\frac{2}{3}$ of 48 is how many sevenths of 28?
5. $\frac{4}{9}$ of 108 is how many fourths of 32?
6. $\frac{7}{15}$ of 90 is how many twelfths of 84?
7. $\frac{3}{20}$ of 160 is how many thirds of 36?
8. $\frac{4}{25}$ of 100 is how many fifteenths of 30?
9. $\frac{3}{4}$ of $10\frac{2}{3}$ is how many sixths of 12?
10. $\frac{7}{6}$ of $37\frac{5}{7}$ is how many tenths of 40?
11. $\frac{3}{8}$ of $42\frac{2}{3}$ is how many ninths of 72?
12. $\frac{4}{5}$ of $78\frac{6}{8}$ is how many thirds of 9?
13. $\frac{2}{3}$ of $28\frac{1}{2}$ is how many halves of 38?
14. $\frac{11}{14}$ of 42 is how many fourths of 44?
15. $\frac{9}{24}$ of 96 is how many fifths of 90?
16. $\frac{11}{5}$ of 40 is how many ninths of 72?

69.   1. $\frac{5}{6}$ of 24 is $\frac{2}{3}$ of what number?

ANALYSIS. $\frac{5}{6}$ *of* 24 *is* $\frac{2}{3}$ *of* 3 *times* $\frac{1}{2}$ *of* 5 *times* $\frac{1}{6}$ *of* 24; $\frac{1}{6}$ *of* 24 *is* 4, 5 *times* 4 *is* 20; $\frac{1}{2}$ *of* 20 *is* 10, *and* 3 *times* 10 *is* 30. *Therefore* $\frac{5}{6}$ *of* 24 *is* $\frac{2}{3}$ *of* 30.

2. $\frac{3}{8}$ of   56 is $\frac{7}{10}$ of what number?
3. $\frac{4}{11}$ of   88 is $\frac{4}{9}$ of what number?
4. $\frac{6}{5}$ of   36 is $\frac{3}{15}$ of what number?
5. $\frac{8}{9}$ of   27 is $\frac{6}{7}$ of what number?
6. $\frac{7}{15}$ of   60 is $\frac{4}{13}$ of what number?
7. $\frac{6}{4}$ of   52 is $\frac{3}{6}$ of what number?
8. $\frac{7}{9}$ of   81 is $\frac{9}{10}$ of what number?
9. $\frac{3}{7}$ of   63 is $\frac{3}{2}$ of what number?
10. $\frac{4}{5}$ of 100 is $\frac{20}{23}$ of what number?
11. $\frac{7}{16}$ of   96 is $\frac{6}{11}$ of what number?
12. $\frac{3}{8}$ of $\frac{2}{3}$ of 64 is $\frac{2}{9}$ of what number?
13. $\frac{4}{5}$ of $\frac{1}{3}$ of 75 is $\frac{10}{17}$ of what number?
14. $\frac{3}{7}$ of $\frac{5}{4}$ of 56 is $\frac{1}{2}$ of $\frac{3}{4}$ of what number?
15. $\frac{5}{9}$ of $\frac{1}{2}$ of 72 is $\frac{1}{4}$ of $\frac{5}{8}$ of what number?
16. $\frac{3}{2}$ of $\frac{5}{6}$ of 36 is $\frac{3}{5}$ of $\frac{1}{2}$ of what number?
17. $\frac{3}{7}$ of 35 is $\frac{5}{8}$ of how many times 7 ?

ANALYSIS. $\frac{3}{7}$ *of* 35 *is* $\frac{5}{8}$ *of as many times* 7 *as* 7 *is contained times in* 8 *times* $\frac{1}{5}$ *of* 3 *times* $\frac{1}{7}$ *of* 35; $\frac{1}{7}$ *of* 35 *is* 5, *and* 3 *times* 5 *is* 15 ; $\frac{1}{5}$ *of* 15 *is* 3, *and* 8 *times* 3 *is* 24 ; 7 *is contained in* 24 $3\frac{3}{7}$ *times. Therefore,* $\frac{3}{7}$ *of* 35 *is* $\frac{5}{8}$ *of* $3\frac{3}{7}$ *times* 7.

18. $\frac{7}{9}$ of   54 is $\frac{6}{5}$ of how many times 5 ?
19. $\frac{5}{4}$ of   24 is $\frac{3}{10}$ of how many times 12 ?
20. $\frac{3}{5}$ of   75 is $\frac{9}{14}$ of how many times 8 ?
21. $\frac{4}{3}$ of   56 is $\frac{2}{5}$ of how many times 20 ?
22. $\frac{3}{9}$ of 108 is $\frac{4}{7}$ of how many times 9 ?

23. $\frac{2}{11}$ of 121 are $\frac{2}{9}$ of how many times 7 ?
24. $\frac{7}{3}$ of 33 are $\frac{7}{5}$ of how many times 6 ?
25. $\frac{12}{17}$ of 34 are $\frac{2}{7}$ of how many times 14 ?
26. $\frac{5}{2}$ of 30 are $\frac{15}{16}$ of how many times 20 ?
27. $\frac{3}{7}$ of $\frac{1}{3}$ of 63 are $\frac{1}{4}$ of $\frac{3}{5}$ of how many times 11 ?
28. $\frac{4}{5}$ of $\frac{3}{4}$ of 50 are $\frac{4}{9}$ of $\frac{1}{3}$ of how many times 8 !

---

70. 1. $\frac{4}{7}$ of 56 are $\frac{8}{9}$ of 3 times what number ?*

ANALYSIS. $\frac{4}{7}$ of 56 are $\frac{8}{9}$ of 3 times $\frac{1}{3}$ of 9 times $\frac{1}{8}$ of 4 times $\frac{1}{4}$ of 56; $\frac{1}{7}$ of 56 is 8, and 4 times 8 is 32; $\frac{1}{8}$ of 32 is 4, and 9 times 4 is 36; $\frac{1}{3}$ of 36 is 12. Therefore, $\frac{4}{7}$ of 56 are $\frac{8}{9}$ of 3 times 12.

2. $\frac{4}{5}$ of 45 are $\frac{6}{7}$ of 6 times what number ?
3. $\frac{5}{8}$ of 64 are $\frac{4}{9}$ of 9 times what number ?
4. $\frac{3}{7}$ of 63 are $\frac{9}{16}$ of 4 times what number ?
5. $\frac{2}{3}$ of 36 are $\frac{3}{10}$ of 5 times what number ?
6. $\frac{4}{11}$ of 110 are $\frac{5}{7}$ of 8 times what number ?
7. $\frac{11}{16}$ of 80 are $\frac{5}{9}$ of 11 times what number ?
8. $\frac{7}{8}$ of 72 are $\frac{9}{10}$ of 5 times what number ?
9. $\frac{8}{9}$ of 81 are $\frac{12}{20}$ of 10 times what number ?
10. $\frac{6}{2}$ of 21 are $\frac{1}{4}$ of 8 times what number ?
11. $\frac{9}{3}$ of 14 are $\frac{6}{7}$ of 3 times what number ?
12. $\frac{3}{4}$ of $\frac{2}{3}$ of 70 are $\frac{5}{12}$ of 4 times what number ?

13. A man, being asked his age, answered that if he were 3 times as old, $\frac{1}{4}$ of his age would be 24 years; how old was he ?

14. A gentleman divided his farm between his 2 sons, giving the elder 10 acres more than $\frac{2}{5}$ of the whole, and the younger the remainder, which was 22 acres more than $\frac{1}{3}$ of the whole; how many acres in the farm ?

* See **70** in the Appendix, page 170.

15. A coal merchant sold $\frac{2}{7}$ of what coal he had on hand for $90, at the rate of $6 a ton ; how many tons had he ?

16. Bought a piano for $300, and $\frac{2}{5}$ of the cost of the instrument was $\frac{4}{3}$ of what I received of 9 young ladies for its use one year ; how much did each young lady pay for its use ?

17. The tools in a shop are worth $80 ; $\frac{3}{4}$ of this is $\frac{2}{3}$ of $\frac{1}{2}$ of 2 times the value of the stock ; what is the value of the stock ?

18. A peddler, after selling $200 worth of his stock in trade, finds that $\frac{6}{7}$ of the remainder is equal to $\frac{5}{6}$ of 3 times the amount sold ; what amount of stock had he at first ?

19. A merchant, after selling from a cask of wine 15 gallons more than $\frac{1}{9}$ of the whole, found that the number of gallons left was just 3 times the number of gallons sold ; how many gallons did the cask contain at first ?

20. If a store be worth $1000, and $\frac{4}{5}$ of the value of the store be equal to $\frac{8}{9}$ of $2\frac{1}{2}$ times the value of the goods it contains, what is the value of the goods ?

21. Two boys, comparing their money, one said he had 50 cents ; the other said, " $\frac{7}{10}$ of your money is just $\frac{5}{12}$ of 6 times my money ; " how many cents had the latter boy ?

22. The distance from Boston to Albany is 200 miles, and $\frac{3}{5}$ of this distance is $\frac{6}{5}$ times $\frac{1}{3}$ the distance from Albany to Niagara Falls, lacking 5 miles ; what is the distance from Boston to Niagara Falls ?

23. The distance from Chicago to Alton is 268 miles, and $\frac{3}{4}$ of this distance plus 15 miles, is $4\frac{1}{2}$ times $\frac{6}{5}$ of the distance from Alton to St. Louis ; what is the distance from Chicago to St. Louis ?

24. 40 is $\frac{2}{3}$ of $\frac{5}{7}$ of $\frac{1}{2}$ of 8 times what number ?

71.   1. $\frac{4}{7}$ of 35 is $\frac{5}{9}$ of how many thirds of 18 ?*

ANALYSIS. *Of as many thirds of* 18 *as* $\frac{1}{3}$ *of* 18 *is contained times in* 9 *times* $\frac{1}{5}$ *of* 4 *times* $\frac{4}{7}$ *of* 35 ; $\frac{1}{7}$ *of* 35 *is* 5, *and* 4 *times* 5 *is* 20 ; $\frac{1}{5}$ *of* 20 *is* 4, *and* 9 *times* 4 *is* 36 ; $\frac{1}{3}$ *of* 18 *is* 6, *and* 6 *is contained in* 36, 6 *times. Therefore,* $\frac{4}{7}$ *of* 35 *is* $\frac{5}{9}$ *of* 6 *thirds of* 18.

2. $\frac{2}{3}$ of   42 is $\frac{4}{7}$ of how many fifths of 35 ?

3. $\frac{3}{8}$ of   96 is $\frac{6}{5}$ of how many eighths of 24 ?

4. $\frac{2}{9}$ of 180 is $\frac{8}{9}$ of how many tenths of 50 ?

5. $\frac{5}{7}$ of   84 is $\frac{3}{4}$ of how many sixths of 48 ?

6. $\frac{7}{20}$ of 100 is $\frac{7}{10}$ of how many ninths of 45 ?

7. $\frac{4}{3}$ of   45 is $\frac{5}{12}$ of how many halves of 48 ?

8. $\frac{6}{11}$ of   77 is $\frac{7}{6}$ of how many twelfths of 72 ?

9. $\frac{11}{15}$ of   30 is $\frac{2}{7}$ of how many thirds of 21 ?

10. $\frac{9}{14}$ of   28 is $\frac{3}{20}$ of how many fourths of 24 ?

11. $\frac{5}{3}$ of   18 is $\frac{6}{11}$ of how many twelfths of 60 ?

12. $\frac{3}{4}$ of   80 is $\frac{2}{3}$ of how many fourths of 40 ?

13. $\frac{9}{7}$ of   42 is $\frac{9}{11}$ of how many eighths of 72 ?

14. $\frac{4}{13}$ of   39 is $\frac{3}{25}$ of how many ninths of 180 ?

15. $\frac{5}{9}$ of $\frac{6}{3}$ of 18 is 4 times what part of 35 ?

ANALYSIS. *Such a part of* 35, *as* 35 *is contained times in* $\frac{1}{4}$ *of* 5 *times* $\frac{1}{9}$ *of* 6 *times* $\frac{1}{3}$ *of* 18 ; $\frac{1}{3}$ *of* 18 *is* 6, *and* 6 *times* 6, *is* 36 ; $\frac{1}{9}$ *of* 36 *is* 4, *and* 5 *times* 4 *is* 20 ; $\frac{1}{4}$ *of* 20 *is* 5, *and* 35 *is contained in* 5, $\frac{5}{35}$ *or* $\frac{1}{7}$ *times. Therefore* $\frac{5}{9}$ *of* $\frac{6}{3}$ *of* 18 *is* 4 *times* $\frac{1}{7}$, *or* $\frac{4}{7}$, *of* 35.

16. $\frac{4}{5}$ of $\frac{3}{8}$ of   40 is 3 times what part of 24 ?

17. $\frac{2}{3}$ of $\frac{3}{7}$ of   49 is 2 times what part of 28 ?

18. $\frac{1}{2}$ of $\frac{9}{10}$ of 100 is 9 times what part of 25 ?

19. $\frac{5}{8}$ of $\frac{7}{6}$ of   48 is 7 times what part of 35 ?

20. $\frac{7}{10}$ of $\frac{2}{3}$ of   60 is 7 times what part of 64 ?

21. $\frac{6}{4}$ of $\frac{2}{5}$ of   80 is 3 times what part of 96 ?

---

* Observe the "changes" in the Appendix, **71**, page 171.

72. 1. $\frac{4}{3}$ of 36 is $\frac{4}{9}$ of how many times $\frac{2}{7}$ of 42?*

ANALYSIS. *Of as many times $\frac{2}{7}$ of 42 as 2 times $\frac{1}{7}$ of 42 is contained times in 9 times $\frac{1}{4}$ of 4 times $\frac{1}{3}$ of 36; $\frac{1}{3}$ of 36 is 12, and 4 times 12 is 48; $\frac{1}{4}$ of 48 is 12, and 9 times 12 is 108; $\frac{1}{7}$ of 42 is 6, and 2 times 6 is 12, and 12 is contained in 108, 9 times. Therefore $\frac{4}{3}$ of 36 is $\frac{4}{9}$ of 9 times $\frac{2}{7}$ of 42.*

2. $\frac{3}{8}$ of 64 is $\frac{4}{6}$ of how many times $\frac{2}{3}$ of 15?

3. $\frac{4}{3}$ of 27 is $\frac{6}{7}$ of how many times $\frac{3}{8}$ of 56?

4. $\frac{7}{9}$ of 81 is $\frac{3}{2}$ of how many times $\frac{1}{4}$ of 28?

5. $\frac{6}{5}$ of 50 is $\frac{10}{12}$ of how many times $\frac{2}{5}$ of 60?

6. $\frac{3}{4}$ of 36 is $\frac{3}{11}$ of how many times $\frac{1}{3}$ of 27?

7. $\frac{5}{8}$ of 32 is $\frac{4}{25}$ of how many times $\frac{5}{9}$ of 45?

8. $\frac{3}{10}$ of 150 is $\frac{3}{4}$ of how many times $\frac{3}{8}$ of 40?

9. $\frac{4}{9}$ of 108 is $\frac{6}{10}$ of how many times $\frac{3}{5}$ of $16\frac{2}{3}$?

10. $\frac{4}{13}$ of 65 is $\frac{1}{7}$ of how many times $\frac{2}{3}$ of $\frac{3}{5}$ of 50?

11. $\frac{3}{5}$ of 60 is $\frac{4}{5}$ of how many times $\frac{6}{5}$ of 25?

12. $\frac{5}{9}$ of 72 is $\frac{2}{6}$ of how many times $\frac{1}{2}$ of $\frac{4}{7}$ of 70?

13. $\frac{2}{3}$ of $\frac{1}{2}$ of 84 is $\frac{4}{9}$ of how many times $\frac{1}{4}$ of $\frac{3}{8}$ of 96?

14. $\frac{4}{6}$ of $\frac{2}{3}$ of 90 is $\frac{1}{2}$ of $\frac{3}{4}$ of how many times $\frac{4}{2}$ of $\frac{2}{5}$ of 20?

15. $\frac{1}{6}$ of $\frac{5}{3}$ of 36 is $\frac{1}{8}$ of $\frac{2}{5}$ of how many times $\frac{2}{3}$ of $\frac{5}{8}$ of 120?

16. A man pays $400 rent, and $\frac{3}{4}$ of this is just $\frac{2}{3}$ of $\frac{1}{2}$ of twice his annual income; what is his annual income?

17. A boy being asked his age said that 18 years was 2 years less than $\frac{3}{4}$ times $\frac{5}{8}$ of his age; how old was he?

18. The distance from Baltimore to Washington is 39 miles; if 5 miles be subtracted from $\frac{2}{3}$ of this

For "changes" see Appendix, **72**, page 178.

distance, the remainder will be $\frac{3}{7}$ times $\frac{1}{2}$ the distance from Philadelphia to Baltimore; what is the distance from Philadelphia to Washington?

19. Mr. B., who is 64 years of age, is $2\frac{2}{3}$ times as old as his eldest son, and his eldest son is $2\frac{2}{5}$ times as old as his youngest brother; what is the difference in the ages of the two brothers?

20. Oscar earned a certain number of pennies; Rufus earned $\frac{4}{5}$ as many minus 4, and David earned $\frac{3}{4}$ as many as Rufus, plus 7; Oscar earned 50 pennies; how many did Rufus and David earn?

21. A man put his money into 4 packages; in the first he put $\frac{2}{6}$, in the second $\frac{1}{3}$, in the third $\frac{1}{6}$, and in the fourth $24; how much money had he?

22. A sold $\frac{1}{5}$ of his sheep on Monday; Tuesday he bought $\frac{3}{4}$ as many as he had sold; he then had 60 sheep; how many had he at first?

23. Mrs. D.'s shawl cost $30; $\frac{4}{5}$ of the cost of the shawl was $\frac{8}{9}$ of 6 times the cost of her dress; what was the cost of her dress?

24. B and C engaging in play, B had $\frac{2}{8}$ as much money as C; C gained $16, which was $\frac{2}{9}$ of $1\frac{1}{2}$ times as much as he commenced with; how much did he commence with, and how much had B left?

25. A farmer, being asked how many sheep he had, replied that he had just sold 150, and that $\frac{4}{5}$ the number he had sold was 6 times $\frac{2}{3}$ of what he had left; how many had he left?

26. Mr. S. gave $\frac{2}{3}$ of $1\frac{1}{5}$ times his ready money for a buggy, $\frac{3}{4}$ of what was left for a harness, and had $12 remaining; what did he pay for the buggy?

27. A paid $4800 for his farm; $\frac{3}{4}$ of this is $4\frac{1}{2}$ times $\frac{4}{9}$ of 2 times what it cost to build the house; what was the cost of the house?

28. $\frac{1}{2}$ of $\frac{3}{5}$ of 80 is $\frac{1}{2}$ of $\frac{2}{5}$ of how many times $\frac{3}{4}$ of $\frac{1}{5}$ of 100?

CHAPTER VII.

RATIO AND PROPORTION.

73.   1. What part of 4 is 1 ? of 4 is 3 ? *

ANALYSIS. *Since* 1 *is* $\frac{1}{4}$ *of* 4, 3 *must be* 3 *times* $\frac{1}{4}$ *part of* 4, *or* $\frac{3}{4}$ *of* 4.   *Therefore* 3 *is* $\frac{3}{4}$ *of* 4.

  2. What part of 3 is 1 ? of 3 is 2 ?
  3. What part of 7 is 1 ? of 5 is 3 ?
  4. What part of 8 is 2 ? of 9 is 5 ?
  5. What part of 10 is 7 ? of 13 is 9 ?
  6. What part of 8 is 9 ? of 12 is 7 ?
  7. What part of 16 is 11 ? of 20 is 17 ?
  8. What part of 40 is 9 ?   What is the ratio ?
  9. What part of 30 is 27 ?   What is the ratio ?
10. What part of $\frac{4}{5}$ is $\frac{2}{3}$?   What is the ratio ?

ANALYSIS. $\frac{4}{5} = \frac{12}{15}$, *and* $\frac{2}{3} = \frac{10}{15}$; *the ratio of* $\frac{10}{15}$ *to* $\frac{12}{15}$ *is the same as that of their numerators,* 10 *to* 12 : *what part of* 12 *is* 10 ? $\frac{10}{12} = \frac{5}{6}$. *Therefore* $\frac{2}{3}$ *is* $\frac{5}{6}$ *of* $\frac{4}{5}$, *and the ratio is* $\frac{5}{6}$.

11. What part of $\frac{3}{4}$ is $\frac{1}{6}$? of $\frac{3}{7}$ is $\frac{1}{6}$?
12. What part of $\frac{7}{8}$ is $\frac{3}{5}$? of $\frac{9}{10}$ is $\frac{1}{2}$?
13. What part of $\frac{6}{7}$ is $\frac{5}{8}$? of $\frac{5}{11}$ is $\frac{2}{3}$?
14. What part of $\frac{7}{12}$ is $\frac{3}{4}$? of $\frac{4}{5}$ is $\frac{2}{7}$?
15. What part of $\frac{9}{14}$ is $\frac{3}{7}$?   What is the ratio ?
16. What part of 5 is $\frac{2}{3}$?   What is the ratio ?
17. What part of 7 is $\frac{5}{6}$? of $3\frac{1}{2}$ is 2 ?
18. What part of $4\frac{1}{3}$ is $\frac{5}{7}$? of $7\frac{1}{2}$ is $3\frac{1}{4}$?
19. What part of $\frac{8}{9}$ is 2 ? of $2\frac{4}{5}$ is $1\frac{2}{3}$?
20. What part of $\frac{7}{10}$ is 5 ? of $\frac{3}{8}$ is 6 ?

---

* The quotient arising from dividing one number by another is called the *ratio*. Thus, what part of 4 is 1 ? It is 1 divided by 4, equal to $\frac{1}{4}$, the *ratio*. What part of 4 is 3 ? It is 3 divided by 4, equal to $\frac{3}{4}$, the *ratio*.

8

74.   1. What part of 25 dollars is 5 dollars ? is 10 dollars ?

2. What part of 16 pounds is 4 pounds ? is 7 pounds ? is 12 pounds ?

3. What part of 1 bushel is 1 peck ? is 2 pecks and 4 quarts ? is 6 quarts ?

4. What part of 1 pound is 12 shillings ?

5. What part of 1 dollar is 20 cents ? is 5 dimes ?

6. What part of 1 cwt. are 15 pounds ?

7. What part of 1 cwt. are 6 lbs. ? 9 lbs. ?

8. What part of 1 ton is 14 cwt. ? 15 cwt. ? 18 cwt. ?

9. What part of 3 pounds is 10 oz. ? is 1 lb. 6 oz. ?

10. What part of 1 foot is 3 in. ? 10 in. ? 11 in. ?

11. What part of 2 yds. is 1 foot ? 1 foot 10 inches ?

12. What part of 1 mile is 3 furlongs ? 5 furlongs 20 rods ?

13. What part of 1 mile is 140 rods ? 160 rods ?

14. What part of 1 gallon is 1 quart ? 1 pint ?

15. What part of 1 hhd. is 5 gallons ? 21 gallons ?

16. What part of 1 quart is 1 pint ? 2 gills ?

17. What part of 1 hour is 15 minutes ? 40 minutes ?

18. What part of 1 day is 3 hours ? 8 hours ? 16 hours ?

19. What part of 3 weeks is 2 days ? 5 days ? 9 days ?

20. What part of 1 year is 3 weeks ? 7 weeks ?

21. What part of 5 pounds 6 ounces is 3 pounds 10 ounces ?

22. What part of 3 hhd. is 1 hhd. 22 gallons ?

23. What part of 1 mile 3 fur. is 4 fur. 20 rods ?

24. What part of 3 pecks is 6 quarts 1 pint ?

25. Two pounds is what part of 1 cwt. ? of 2 cwt. ?

26. Eight inches is what part of a foot ? of 2 feet ? of 1 yard ? of 4 yards ?

27. Three quarts is what part of a gallon ? of 5 gallons ? of 10 gallons ? of 1 hhd. ?

28. What part of 9 miles is $\frac{3}{4}$ of 8 miles ?

29. What part of $4\frac{1}{2}$ acres is $\frac{1}{3}$ of $3\frac{1}{4}$ acres ?

30. A man, having $15, gave. 3\frac{1}{2}$ for a hat, and 4\frac{1}{3}$ for a pair of boots ; what part of his money did he use, and what part had he left ?

31. A farmer, having 160 bushels of wheat, sold $\frac{1}{2}$ of $\frac{3}{4}$ of it, floured $\frac{2}{5}$ of $\frac{7}{8}$ of it, and kept the remainder for seed ; what part of the whole did he use for each purpose ?

32. If I have sold $\frac{2}{3}$ of $\frac{4}{5}$ of 120 sheep, what part of the whole flock have I left ?

33. One man can walk $4\frac{3}{4}$ miles while another walks $3\frac{2}{5}$ miles ; what part of the distance that the first walks does the second walk ?

34. A gentleman paid $\frac{5}{7}$ of 39\frac{1}{5}$ for a coat, and 9\frac{1}{3}$ for a pair of pantaloons ; how many times as much did he pay for the coat as for the pantaloons ?

35. Paid 7\frac{2}{3}$ for a barrel of flour, and $1\frac{4}{5}$ times as much for a ton of hay ; what was the cost of the hay ?

36. A man bought a horse for $225, and a carriage for $\frac{1}{3}$ of $\frac{3}{4}$ of this sum ; what part of $125 did the carriage cost ?

37. If a vessel sail 40 miles in 5 hours, what part of 144 miles will she sail in 9 hours ? how many miles ?

38. A man gave to his 3 sons 360 acres of western land ; to the first he gave $\frac{3}{8}$ of it, to the second $\frac{2}{9}$ of $3\frac{1}{2}$ times as much, and the remainder he gave to the third ; what part of the whole did each receive ? how many acres ?

39. A merchant gained on a hogshead of sugar $\frac{4}{5}$ of 46\frac{2}{3}$, which was $\frac{1}{3}$ of 2 times what it cost him ; what did it cost him ? what part of the cost was the gain ?

75.   1. If 6 cords of wood cost $15, what will 4 cords cost?

ANALYSIS. *Four cords are* $\frac{4}{6}$, *or* $\frac{2}{3}$ *of* 6 *cords. If* 6 *cords of wood cost* $15, 4 *cords will cost* $\frac{2}{3}$ *of* $15; $\frac{1}{3}$ *of* $15 *is* $5, *and* $\frac{2}{3}$ *of* $15 *is* 2 *times* $5, *or* $10. *Therefore, &c.*

Or, *the pupil may use the form of analysis used in section* **22,** *on page* 41.

2. If 9 pounds of sugar cost 75 cents, what will 12 pounds cost?

3. If 6 men can cut 45 cords of wood in 3 days, how many cords can 8 men cut in the same time?

4. If $3\frac{1}{2}$ yards of cloth cost $10\frac{1}{2}$, how much will 7 yards cost?

5. If $4\frac{2}{5}$ pounds of butter cost 66 cents, what will $2\frac{2}{3}$ pounds cost?

6. If a mechanic earn $13\frac{1}{2}$ shillings in $1\frac{1}{2}$ days, how much can he earn in a week?

7. If $7\frac{1}{4}$ will buy $3\frac{1}{4}$ cords of wood, how many cords can be bought for $10\frac{1}{2}$?

8. If $\frac{1}{2}$ barrel of flour cost $4\frac{1}{2}$, what will $\frac{2}{3}$ of a barrel cost?

ANALYSIS. *What part of* $\frac{1}{2}$ *is* $\frac{2}{3}$? $\frac{1}{2} = \frac{3}{6}$, *and* $\frac{2}{3} = \frac{4}{6}$; *the ratio of* $\frac{4}{6}$ *to* $\frac{3}{6}$ *is the same as of* 3 *to* 4, $= \frac{4}{3}$. *Then, since* $\frac{1}{2}$ *barrel of flour cost* $4\frac{1}{2}$, $\frac{2}{3}$ *of a barrel will cost* $\frac{4}{3}$ *of* $4\frac{1}{2}$; $\frac{4}{3}$ *of* $\frac{9}{2} = \frac{36}{6} = $6. *Therefore, &c.*

9. If a man can run 6 miles in $\frac{3}{2}$ of an hour, how far can he run in $3\frac{1}{4}$ hours?

10. How many yards of carpeting $\frac{2}{3}$ of a yard wide are equal to 12 yards $\frac{3}{4}$ of a yard wide?

11. If a staff 3 feet long cast a shadow 5 feet in length, what would be the length of the shadow cast by a pole 13 feet long?

12. If the sawing of $\frac{6}{7}$ of a cord of wood cost $6\frac{1}{2}$ shillings, what would the sawing of $3\frac{3}{7}$ cords cost?

13. John earns 9 cents as often as James earns 15 cents; when John has earned 63 cents, how much has James earned?

14. Two persons start from different points and travel towards each other; the first one travels 7 miles while the other travels 5 miles, and when they meet the first one has traveled 70 miles; how far apart were they when they started?

15. If 4 men can build a wall 60 feet long in 6 days, in what time can 3 men build a wall 90 feet in length?

ANALYSIS. *In $\frac{4}{3}$ of $\frac{90}{60}$ of 6 days, which are 12 days. Or thus: if it will take 4 men 6 days to build a wall 60 feet long, it will take 1 man 4 times 6 days, or 24 days, and 3 men can do it in $\frac{1}{3}$ of 24, or 8 days; to build a wall 1 foot long will require $\frac{1}{60}$ of 8, or $\frac{8}{60}$ days, and to build a wall 90 feet long will require 90 times as many days, or 90 times $\frac{8}{60}$, equal to 12 days. Therefore, &c.*

16. If 5 men can do a piece of work in 10 days, how many men will do a piece of work 4 times as large in 20 days?

17. If a man perform a journey in 8 days, by traveling 9 hours a day, how many days will he require to perform the same journey, if he travel 12 hours a day?

18. If 5 horses eat $1\frac{1}{2}$ tons of hay in 1 month, how many tons will 6 horses eat in $2\frac{2}{3}$ months?

19. How many days will it take 5 men to earn $11\frac{2}{3}$, if 3 men earn $\frac{7}{8}$ in $\frac{1}{4}$ of a day?

20. If 1 horse eat $1\frac{1}{2}$ bushels of oats in 3 days, in how many days will 4 horses eat 49 bushels?

21. If a barrel of flour will supply a family of 4 persons 5 weeks, how much will supply a family of 3 persons $2\frac{1}{2}$ weeks?

22. If 3 furnaces consume $12\frac{1}{4}$ tons of coal in 7 days, how long will $17\frac{1}{2}$ tons last 5 furnaces?

76.   CHAPTER VIII.

PERCENTAGE.

THE terms, *percentage* and *per cent.*, signify *by the hundred*, or *hundredths*, that is, a certain number of parts of each *one hundred* parts, of whatever denomination. Thus, by 5 per cent. is meant 5 cents of every 100 cents, $5 of every $100, 5 bushels of every 100 bushels, &c. Therefore, 5 per cent. equals 5 hundredths, ($\frac{5}{100}$,) or $\frac{1}{20}$. 8 per cent., 8 hundredths, ($\frac{8}{100}$,) or $\frac{2}{25}$ of the given number or quantity.

1. A man, having $40, lost 3 per cent. of it; how many dollars did he lose?

ANALYSIS. *Since he lost* 3 *per cent., or* $\frac{3}{100}$, *on* $1, *on* $40 *he lost* 40 *times* $\frac{3}{100}$, *or* $\frac{120}{100}$ *of* $1, *equal to* $1\frac{1}{5}$. *Therefore, &c.*

2. What is 5 per cent. of $25? of $30? of $45?
3. What is 7 per cent. of $15? ot $40? of $200?
4. What is 6 per cent. of $18? of $37? of $54?
5. What is 3 per cent. of 50 bushels of corn?
6. What is 10 per cent. of 160 tons of plaster?
7. What is 25 per cent. of 96 gallons of wine?
8. What is 12 per cent. of 33½ pounds of sugar?
9. What is 15 per cent. of 110 barrels of flour?
10. What is 8 per cent. of 28 yards of cloth?
11. What is $\frac{2}{3}$ per cent. of $45?

ANALYSIS. *Since* 1 *per cent of* $45 *is* $\frac{45}{100}$, $\frac{2}{3}$ *of* 1 *per cent. is* $\frac{2}{3}$ *of* $\frac{45}{100}$, *or* $\frac{30}{100}$, *equal to* $\frac{3}{10}$. *Therefore, &c.*

12. What is $\frac{3}{4}$ per cent. of $28? of $44? of $56?
13. What is $\frac{1}{3}$ per cent. of $63? of $120?
14. What is $\frac{2}{5}$ per cent. of 30 barrels of cider?
15. What is 3½ per cent of 70 sheep? of 35 cows?
16. What is 2⅛ per cent. of 34 hundred weight?

17. A man bought 75 barrels of apples, and on opening them, found 8 per cent. of them spoiled; how many barrels did he lose?

18. If I have $200 deposited in the bank, and draw out 15 per cent. of it, how much remains?

19. A farmer, having 176 sheep, sold 75 per cent. of them, and kept the remainder; how many did he keep?

20. A young man, having $104, lost $12\frac{1}{2}$ per cent. of it in gambling; how many dollars did he lose, and what per cent. of the whole had he left?

---

77.   1. What fraction of a number is 8 per cent. of it?

ANALYSIS. *Since* 1 *per cent. is* $\frac{1}{100}$, 8 *per cent. is* 8 *times* $\frac{1}{100}$, *or* $\frac{8}{100}$, $= \frac{2}{25}$. *Therefore* 8 *per cent. equals* $\frac{2}{25}$ *of any number or thing.*

2. What fraction of a number is 6 per cent.? 7 per cent.? 10 per cent.? $12\frac{1}{2}$ per cent.?

3. What fraction of a number is $6\frac{1}{4}$ per cent.? $16\frac{2}{3}$ per cent.? 20 per cent.? $37\frac{1}{2}$ per cent.? 40 per cent.?

4. If you have $120, and lose $33\frac{1}{3}$ per cent. of it, what part of it will you lose?

5. James, having 250 marbles, lost 40 per cent. of them at play; what part of the whole had he left, and how many did he lose?

6. What per cent. of a barrel of flour is $\frac{2}{5}$ of it?

ANALYSIS. *Since the whole of any number or thing is equal to* 100 *per cent.*, $\frac{2}{5}$ *of one barrel of flour is equal to* $\frac{2}{5}$ *of* 100 *per cent., or* 40 *per cent. Therefore, &c.*

7. If a man save $\frac{5}{8}$ of his income, what per cent. does he spend?

8. If a merchant invest $\frac{2}{5}$ of his money in dry goods, what per cent. does he invest?

78. 1. A farmer, having 20 sheep, lost 5 of them by disease; what per cent. did he lose?

ANALYSIS. *Since* 20 *sheep are* 100 *per cent., or all that he had,* 5 *sheep are* $\frac{5}{20}$, *or* $\frac{1}{4}$, *of all he had; and* $\frac{1}{4}$ *of* 100 *per cent. is* 25 *per cent. Therefore, &c.*

2. What per cent. of 21 is 7?

3. What per cent. of 50 is 5? 10? 20? 25?

4. What per cent. of $40 is $5? $8? $25? $30?

5. What per cent. of 18 pounds is 3 pounds? 12 pounds?

6. What per cent. of 42 miles is 6 miles? 7 miles?

7. What per cent. of $12\frac{1}{2}$ is $2\frac{1}{2}$? $6\frac{1}{4}$?

8. What per cent. of 30 is 12? 15? 20?

9. What per cent. of 18 is 9? 12? 15?

10. $1\frac{1}{2}$ is what per cent. of 9? of 15? of 21?

11. $2\frac{1}{2}$ is what per cent. of $7\frac{1}{2}$? of $12\frac{1}{2}$? of 10?

12. $\frac{1}{3}$ is what per cent. of $3\frac{1}{3}$? of $16\frac{2}{3}$? of 20?

13. $\frac{12}{5}$ is what per cent. of 8? of 12? of 20?

14. If from a hogshead of molasses a grocer draw 42 gallons, what per cent. of the whole will remain?

15. From a box of tea containing 60 pounds, 15 pounds were sold at one time, and 25 pounds at another; what per cent. of the whole remained unsold?

16. In a heap of potatoes containing 150 bushels, 3 bushels of every 5 are bad; what per cent. are bad, and how many bushels are good?

17. A gambler, having $250, lost $80 at play; what per cent. of his money did he lose, and what per cent. had he left?

18. James, having $62\frac{1}{2}$ cents, gave $37\frac{1}{2}$ for a book; what per cent. of his money had he left?

19. A grocer, having a barrel of sugar containing 200 pounds, sold $\frac{1}{4}$ of it at one time, and $\frac{1}{3}$ of the remainder at another time; what per cent. remained unsold?

79. 1. A person collects $240, and receives 5 per cent. commission on what he collects; what compensation does he receive?

ANALYSIS. *Since the commission is 5 per cent., or $\frac{5}{100}$, equal to $\frac{1}{20}$, of the sum collected, he receives $\frac{1}{20}$ of $240, which is $12. Therefore, &c.*

2. What will be the expense of collecting a note of $800, at 10 per cent. commission?

3. What must be paid for collecting a tax of $300, allowing $12\frac{1}{2}$ per cent. commission?

4. An agent sells $1200 worth of merchandise, at 25 per cent. commission; how much will he receive for his services?

5. An auctioneer sold goods to the amount of $500; what will his commission amount to, at $2\frac{1}{2}$ per cent.?

6. Paid an attorney $3\frac{1}{8}$ per cent. to collect a debt of $640; how much did he receive for his services?

7. If a man fail in business, and can pay but 40 per cent. of his debts, how much will a creditor receive on a debt of $175?

8. Bought $1000 worth of books, receiving a commission of $3\frac{3}{5}$ per cent.; how much did I receive for my services?

9. If a broker sell $600 worth of New York Central Railroad stock, and charge $\frac{3}{4}$ per cent. for selling, how much will he receive?

10. At $\frac{4}{5}$ of 1 per cent., what will be the expense of negotiating a bill of exchange of $625?

11. A broker in Chicago exchanged $1200 on the Chemical Bank of New York, at $\frac{3}{8}$ per cent.; what amount of brokerage did he receive?

12. A real estate agent sells a house and lot for $2000, and charges $1\frac{1}{3}$ per cent. commission for selling; how much does he receive?

80. 1. A merchant sends his agent $780 to expend for merchandise, after deducting his commission of 4 per cent.; what sum will he expend?

ANALYSIS. *The money to be expended is* $\frac{100}{100}$ *of itself, and the commission* $\frac{4}{100}$, *or* $\frac{1}{25}$, *of this sum; hence the whole amount sent to the agent is* $\frac{104}{100}$, *or* $\frac{26}{25}$. *Since* $780 *is* $\frac{26}{25}$, $\frac{1}{25}$ *is* $\frac{1}{26}$ *of* $780, *or* $30, *his commission; and* $\frac{25}{25}$ *is 25 times 30, or* $750, *the sum to be expended.*

2. I gave a broker $810 to invest in bank stock, after deducting his commission of 1¼ per cent.; what was his commission, and how much did he invest?

3. A distiller sent Mr. B. $1550, with which to buy corn, after deducting his commission of 3⅓ per cent.; how much did he expend, and how much did his commission amount to?

4. How many bushels of wheat, at $1 a bushel, can an agent buy for $1230, and retain 2½ per cent. commission for his trouble?

5. A farmer employed a man to thresh his wheat, agreeing to give him 12 per cent. of all he threshed; how many bushels must he thresh that the farmer may retain 66 bushels?

ANALYSIS. *Since the thresher received* $\frac{12}{100}$, *or* $\frac{3}{25}$ *of all he threshed, the farmer received the difference between* $\frac{100}{100}$, *or* $\frac{25}{25}$ *and* $\frac{3}{25}$, *which is* $\frac{22}{25}$. *Then 66 bushels is* $\frac{22}{25}$ *of the whole number of bushels threshed; since 66 bushels is* $\frac{22}{25}$, $\frac{1}{25}$ *is* $\frac{1}{22}$ *of 66, or 3 bushels, and* $\frac{25}{25}$ *is 25 times 3 bushels, or 75 bushels. Therefore, &c.*

6. What amount must be collected on a rate bill, that the collector may retain his fee of 5 per cent., and pay over $228?

7. What amount of accounts must an individual collect in order to pay over $1100, and retain 8⅓ per cent. for collecting?

81. 1. What must be paid for insuring a house
and furniture for $1000, at 1¼ per cent. premium ? *

ANALYSIS. *Since the premium is* 1¼ *per cent., or* $\frac{5}{400}$,
equal to $\frac{1}{80}$ *of the amount insured, the premium on* $1000
will be $\frac{1}{80}$ *of* $1000, *or* $12½. *Therefore, &c.*

2. What will be the premium for insuring 200
barrels of flour, valued at $1200, at 4 per cent. ?

3. What must I pay annually for an insurance of
$900 upon my life, at 2½ per cent. ?

4. What must be paid for insuring a case of cloths,
valued at $600, at 1⅖ per cent. premium ?

5. What is the annual premium of insurance, at
¾ per cent., on a building valued at $4000 ?

6. If a merchant has his stock of goods insured
for $2500, at ⅘ of 1 per cent., what is the premium ?

7. A man owns ¾ of a boat load of grain, valued
at $1600, and insures his interest at 1⅔ per cent;
what premium does he pay ?

8. At 2 per cent., what amount of insurance can
I obtain for $18 premium ?

ANALYSIS. *Since 2 per cent. premium is* $\frac{2}{100}$, *or* $\frac{1}{50}$ *of
the amount insured,* $18, *the given premium, will be equal
to* $\frac{1}{50}$ *of the required amount of insurance;* $18 *is* $\frac{1}{50}$ *of* 50
times $18, *equal to* $900. *Therefore, &c.*

9. At 3 per cent., what amount of insurance can
be obtained on a house for $75 ?

10. At ¾ per cent., what amount of insurance can
be obtained on a boat load of flour, for $24 ?

11. What amount of insurance can be had for
$45, upon a car load of horses, at 4½ per cent. ?

12. If the rate is 1¾ per cent., and the premium
paid is $91, what will be the amount of insurance
obtained on a store and its contents ?

---

* The sum paid for insurance is called the *premium.*

82. 1. If a man buy a horse for $90, for how much must he sell him to gain 20 per cent. ?

ANALYSIS. *Since he gains* 20 *per cent., or* $\frac{20}{100}$*, equal to* $\frac{1}{5}$ *of what the horse cost him, he must sell him for* $\frac{6}{5}$ *of what he cost;* $\frac{1}{5}$ *of* $90 *is* $18, *and* $\frac{6}{5}$ *of* $90 *is* 6 *times* $18, *or* $108. *Therefore, &c.*

2. A sleigh was bought for $50, and sold for 8 per cent. more than it cost; what was it sold for ?

3. Bought a quantity of sugar for $84, and sold it at an advance of $12\frac{1}{2}$ per cent; what was it sold for?

4. A grocer bought some tea for $45, but finding it damaged, he was obliged to sell it at a loss of 10 per cent.; what did he sell it for ?

5. Paid $12 for 15 yards of cloth; what must it be sold for a yard to gain 25 per cent. ?

6. A drover bought 60 sheep for $180, and sold them at a loss of 20 per cent. on the cost; what did he receive per head for them ?

7. A grocer bought 440 lemons for $12, and after throwing away 10 per cent. of them, lacking 4, as worthless, he sold the remainder so as to gain $33\frac{1}{3}$ per cent. on the cost of the whole; what did he sell them for apiece ?

8. Bought 6 barrels of flour for $40; for what must it be sold a barrel to gain 5 per cent. on the cost ?

9. If I buy eggs at 10 cents a dozen, how must I sell them to gain 30 per cent. ?

10. A speculator bought a quantity of pork for $500, and sold it at a loss of 7 per cent.; with the proceeds he bought another quantity, upon which he gained 20 per cent.; what was his gain on the whole ?

11. Bought hay at $14 dollars a ton, which was $12\frac{1}{2}$ per cent. less than the market price; what was the market price ?

83. 1. What is gained per cent. by selling clover seed for $6, that cost $4 ?

ANALYSIS. *The whole gain is equal to the difference between $6 and $4, which is $2. Since $4 gain $2, or ½ of itself, equal to $\frac{50}{100}$, the gain will be 50 per cent. Therefore, &c.*

2. What per cent. is gained by selling pork for $7 a hundred weight, that cost $6 ?

3. What will be gained by expending $500 for sugar, when it can be bought for 8 cents, and sold for 8½ cents a pound ?

4. If I buy $300 worth of sheep, and sell them for $375, what do I gain per cent. ?

5. Mr. C. bought a horse for $153, and sold him for $128 ; what per cent. did he lose ?

6. A grocer bought eggs for 9 cents a dozen, and sold them for 12 cents ; what per cent. did he gain ?

7. What per cent. is lost in buying corn at 50 cents a bushel, and selling it at 45 cents ?

8. If a house bring ½ of its value every 4 years in rent, what is the gain per cent. each year ?

9. Bought a horse for 20 per cent. less than $150, and sold him for 10 per cent more than $150 ; what per cent. was gained ?

10. A peddler bought oranges for 18 cents a dozen, and sold them for 2 cents each ; what per cent. did he gain ?

11. A farmer refused to sell his barley for 75 cents a bushel, and was afterwards obliged to take 60 cents a bushel for it ; what per cent. did he lose ?

12. Bought cotton cloth at 7½ cents a yard, and sold it for 9 cents a yard ; what was the gain per cent. ?

13. Sold damaged cloth so as to lose ⅓ of what it cost ; what per cent. was lost ?

84. 1. A tailor sold a coat for $24, by which he gained 20 per cent. on the first cost; what was its cost?

ANALYSIS. *Since he gained* 20 *per cent., or* $\frac{1}{5}$ *of the cost,* $24 *is* $\frac{6}{5}$ *of the cost; since* $24 *is* $\frac{6}{5}$, $\frac{1}{6}$ *of* $24, *or* $4, *is* $\frac{1}{5}$ *of the cost, and* $4 *is* $\frac{1}{5}$ *of* 5 *times* $4, *or* $20. *Therefore, &c.*

2. A hatter sold a hat for $$3\frac{1}{2}$, which was $12\frac{1}{2}$ per cent. above cost; what did it cost?

3. A jeweler sold a watch for $65, thereby gaining 30 per cent. on its cost; what was its cost?

4. A mechanic sold a carriage for $108, which was 10 per cent. less than it cost; how much would he have received for it had he sold it so as to gain 20 per cent.?

5. If $16\frac{2}{3}$ per cent. is gained by selling flour at $7 a barrel, what did it cost?

6. A merchant sold 2 barrels of sugar for $24 each; on one barrel he gained 20 per cent. and on the other he lost 20 per cent.; did he gain or lose by the bargain, and how much?

7. A grocer bought coffee so that he could sell it for 18 cents a pound, and make a profit of $33\frac{1}{3}$ per cent.; what did it cost him?

8. A man bought a horse and carriage; he sold them both at 8 per cent. above cost, receiving $81 for the horse, and $108 for the carriage; what was the cost of both?

9. A fruit dealer sold pine-apples at 96 cents a dozen, thereby losing 4 per cent.; what did they cost apiece?

10. B sells a horse to C, and gains $12\frac{1}{2}$ per cent.; C sells him to D for $118, and thereby gains 18 per cent.; how much did the horse cost B?

85. 1. Sold wheat so as to gain 16 cents on a bushel, which was $12\frac{1}{2}$ per cent. of what it cost; what did it cost?

2. A broker exchanged $150 at $\frac{1}{3}$ per cent.; how much brokerage did he receive?

3. A man, having a farm of 200 acres, sold 75 acres of it; what per cent. of the whole remains unsold?

4. What per cent. does William gain by selling apples at $\frac{1}{6}$ of the cost?

5. If I buy stoves at $12 each, and sell them at $8\frac{1}{3}$ per cent. profit, what will I gain on 1 stove?

6. If a broker buy $800 worth of bank stock for me, and charge $\frac{1}{4}$ per cent. brokerage, how much will he receive?

7. Sold butter so as to gain $\frac{2}{5}$ as much as it cost; what per cent. was gained?

8. Mr. A. lends his money so as to receive a sum equal to $\frac{1}{10}$ of it for its use; what per cent. does he receive?

9. A brewer sends a person $520 with which to purchase barley, after deducting his commission of 4 per cent.; how much does he expend, and how much does his commission amount to?

10. The cost of building a town house, and paying collector's fees of 5 per cent., was $945; what was the cost of the house?

11. Hiram agrees to dig farmer F.'s potatoes for 8 per cent. of what should be put into the farmer's cellar; he digs 324 bushels; how many bushels should be put into the cellar, and how many bushels should Hiram receive?

12. Bought $200 worth of dry goods, and $300 worth of groceries; on the dry goods I lost 20 per cent., but on the groceries I gained 15 per cent.; did I gain or lose on my whole capital, and how much?

13. A merchant bought 40 bushels of grass seed, at the rate of 4 bushels for $6, and sold it at the rate of 5 bushels for $8; what was his whole gain, and what his gain per cent.?

14. A drover bought 20 sheep for $50, and sold them so as to gain 20 per cent.; how much did he receive a head for them?

15. A man bought 60 cords of wood for $200, and sold it at a loss of 5 per cent.; at what price did he sell it per cord?

16. If I buy rice at 4 cents a pound, and sell it at 5 cents, what is my gain per cent.?

17. Sold a cow at auction for $18 that cost $20; what was the loss per cent.?

18. A boy bought peaches at the rate of 3 for 2 cents, and sold them at the rate of 9 for 7 cents; what was his gain per cent.?

19. A tailor sold two coats for $26 each; on one he gained 30 per cent., and on the other he lost 30 per cent.; did he gain or lose on both, and how much?

20. A music dealer sold a piano-forte for $230, which was 8 per cent. less than its value; had he sold it for $300, what would have been his gain per cent.?

21. Two men buy a lot of pork together; A furnishes $200, and B $150; their profits are $70; what is their gain per cent., and what is each one's share of the gain?

22. If a ton of hay is bought for $\frac{4}{5}$ of the market price, and sold for 5 per cent. more than the market price, what per cent. is gained?

23. A person engaged in speculation sold out his interest for $2100, which was 30 per cent. less than twice as much money as he began with; how much did he begin with, and what was his gain?

86. INTEREST is a sum paid for the use of borrowed money, or on demands after they become due.

The PRINCIPAL is the *money lent*, or the sum for which interest is paid.

The AMOUNT is the sum of the *principal* and *interest*.

The RATE PER CENT. is the sum paid for the use of $100 or 100 cents for one year. Thus, if $6 be paid for the use of $100 one year, the rate is 6 per cent. per annum.

The interest on any sum for one year is always a certain number of *hundredths* of the *principal*. Thus, the interest of any sum for one year, at 5 per cent., is 5 *hundredths* ($\frac{5}{100}$) or $\frac{1}{20}$ of the *principal*; at 8 per cent. it is 8 *hundredths* ($\frac{8}{100}$) or $\frac{2}{25}$ of the *principal*.

Practically, 30 days are considered a month, and 12 months a year, in computing interest. When no time is named, *one year* is always understood.

The *rate* of interest is established by law; and taking more than such rates is termed *usury*.

1. What is the yearly interest of $80, at 5 per cent.?

ANALYSIS. *Since the interest is 5 per cent., or $\frac{5}{100}$, equal to $\frac{1}{20}$ of the principal, the interest of $80 is $\frac{1}{20}$ of $80, or $4. Therefore, &c.*

Or thus : *Since the interest of $1, or 100 cents, is 5 cents for one year, the interest of $80 is 80 times 5 cents, or 400 cents, equal to $4.**

2. What is the yearly interest of $200, at 6 per cent.?

3. What is the yearly interest of $125, at 4 per cent.?   •

4. What is the annual interest of $60, at 7 per cent.?

5. What is the annual interest of $95, at 5 per cent.?

---

* The *fractional* method is considered preferable in mental exercises.

6. What is the annual interest of $26, at 10 per
cent. ?

7. What is the annual interest of $228, at 12½
per cent. ?

8. What is the annual interest of $96.32, at 6¼
per cent. ?

9. What is the annual interest of $144.60, at 8⅓
per cent. ?

10. What is the annual interest of $400, at 15
per cent. ?

11. What is the annual interest of $500, at 7
per cent. ?

12. What is the annual interest of $120.80, at 7½
per cent. ?

13. What is the annual interest of $1000, at 9
per cent. ?

14. What is the annual interest of $150, at 3 per
cent. ?

---

87. 1. What is the interest of $150 for 3 years,
at 8 per cent. ?

ANALYSIS. *Since the interest for* 1 *year at* 8 *per cent.
is* $\frac{8}{100}$, *equal to* $\frac{2}{25}$, *of the principal, for* 3 *years it is* 3
times $\frac{2}{25}$, *or* $\frac{6}{25}$, *of the principal.* $\frac{2}{25}$ *of* $150 *is* $6, *and*
$\frac{6}{25}$ *of* $150 *is* 6 *times* $6, *or* $36. *Therefore, &c.*

Or thus : *Since the interest of* $150 *for* 1 *year at* 8 *per
cent. is* $12, (**86,**) *for* 3 *years it is* 3 *times* $12, *or* $36.

2. What is the interest of $30 for 2 years, at 5
per cent. ?

3. What is the interest of $50 for 4 years, at 6
per cent. ?

4. What is the interest of $90 for 5 years, at 7
per cent. ?

5. What is the interest of $75 for 3 years, at 12
per cent. ?

6. What is the interest of $64.96 for 2 years, at 6¼ per cent. ?

7. A's note of $25 has been due 2 years; what is the interest, at 6 per cent. ?

8. Borrowed $300 for 3 years, at 7 per cent.; what will be the interest?

9. What is the interest on a note of $46.50, for 5 years, at 10 per cent. ?

10. I owe two notes, one for $145, due in 2 years, at 5 per cent., and the other for $200, due in 3 years, at 6 per cent.; what will be the sum of the interest that I must pay?

11. What is the interest of $225 for 2 years, at 7 per cent. ?

12. What is the interest of $50 for 8 years, at 6 per cent. ?

13. What is the interest of $400 for 2 years, at 5½ per cent. ?

14. Gave a note for $88.96, due in 3 years, at 6¼ per cent; what will be the interest?

15. Gave a note due at date, for $45.50, but did not pay it until the end of 5 years; what was the interest due, at 8 per cent. ?

---

88. 1. At 8 per cent., what part of $1 equals the use of it for 3 years 9 months?

ANALYSIS. *Since there are* 12 *months in* 1 *year,* 9 *months is* $\frac{9}{12}$, *or* ¾ *of* 1 *year, and* 3 *years* 9 *months are equal to* 3¾, *or* $\frac{15}{4}$ *years. Since the interest of* $1 *for* 1 *year at* 8 *per cent. is* $\frac{8}{100}$, *equal to* $\frac{2}{25}$ *of the principal, for* 3 *years* 9 *months, it is* 3¾ *times, or* $\frac{15}{4}$, *of* $\frac{2}{25}$, *equal to* $\frac{3}{10}$ *of the principal, or* $\frac{3}{10}$. *Therefore, &c.*

2. At 6 per cent., what part of $1 equals the use of it for 2 years 8 months?

3. At 5 per cent., what part of any sum equals the use of it for 2 years 6 months?

4. At 7 per cent., what part of any sum equals the interest of it for 1 year 8 months?

5. What part of any sum equals the interest of it for 3 years 2 months, at 4 per cent. ?

6. What part of any sum equals the interest of it for 5 years 4 months, at 9 per cent. ?

7. At $6\frac{1}{4}$ per cent., for 3 years 4 months, what part of the principal equals the interest?

8. At 8 per cent., for 5 years 5 months, what part of the principal equals the interest?

9. At $7\frac{1}{2}$ per cent., for 2 years 11 months, what part of the principal equals the interest?

10. At 6 per cent., for 2 years 1 month, what part of the principal equals the interest?

11. At 10 per cent., for 4 years 10 months, what part of the principal equals the interest?

12. At 8 per cent., for 3 years 3 months and 18 days, what part of the principal equals the interest?

ANALYSIS. *Since* 30 *days make a month,* 18 *days are* $\frac{18}{30}$, *or* $\frac{3}{5}$ *of a month; and since* 12 *months make a year,* 1 *month is* $\frac{1}{12}$ *of a year;* $\frac{1}{5}$ *of* 1 *month is* $\frac{1}{5}$ *of* $\frac{1}{12}$, *or* $\frac{1}{60}$ *of* 1 *year, and* $3\frac{3}{5}$ *months, equal to* $\frac{18}{5}$, *is* 18 *times* $\frac{1}{60}$, *or* $\frac{3}{10}$ *of a year. Hence the interest of* $1 *for* $3\frac{3}{10}$, *or* $\frac{33}{10}$ *years, at* 8 *per cent., is* $\frac{33}{125}$ *of it.* (88, *Ex.* 1.) *Therefore, &c.*

13. What part of the principal equals the interest, for 2 years 5 months and 10 days, at 6 per cent. ?

14. What part of the principal equals the interest, for 1 year 8 months and 25 days, at 7 per cent. ?

15. What part of the principal equals the interest, for 2 years 3 months and 6 days, at 6 per cent. ?

16. What part of the principal equals the interest, for 2 years 11 months and 6 days, at 5 per cent. ?

17. At 7½ per cent., for 8 months 10 days, what part of the principal will equal the interest?

18. At 6 per cent., for 5 years 7 months and 15 days, what part of the principal will equal the interest?

19. At 8⅓ per cent., for 3 years 5 months and 12 days, what part of the principal equals the interest?

20. At 7 per cent., for 11 months 3 days, what part of the principal will equal the interest?

21. At 4 per cent., for 8 years 6 months and 15 days, what part of the principal will equal the interest?

---

89. 1. What is the interest of $40 for 3 years 4 months, at 6 per cent.?

ANALYSIS. *3 years 4 months equals* 3⅓, *or* $\frac{10}{3}$ *years; and the interest of any sum for* $\frac{10}{3}$ *years, at 6 per cent., equals* ⅕ *of it. (88.)* ⅕ *of $40 is $8, the required interest. Therefore, &c.*

Or thus: *Since the interest of $1 for 1 year, at 6 per cent., is 6 cents, for $40 it is 40 times 6 cents, or $2.40, and for* 3⅓ *years it is* 3⅓ *times $2.40, equal to $8.*

2. What is the interest of $150 for 2 years 10 months, at 8 per cent.?

3. What is the interest of $80.40 for 4 years 2 months, at 7 per cent.?

4. What is the interest of $240 for 1 year 9 months, at 5 per cent.?

5. What is the interest of $120 for 5 years 8 months, at 7½ per cent.?

6. What is the interest of $90 for 4 years 7 months, at 4 per cent.?

7. What is the interest of $500 for 10 months, at 6 per cent.?

8. What is the interest of $128 for 2 years 9 months, at 6¼ per cent. ?

9. What is the interest of $125 for 1 year 4 months, at 7 per cent. ?

10. What is the interest of $300 for 8 months, at 6 per cent. ?

11. What is the interest of $50 for 5 years 7 months and 15 days, at 8 per cent. ?

ANALYSIS. *The interest of any sum for 5 years 7 months and 15 days, at 8 per cent., equals $\frac{9}{20}$ of it, (88, Ex. 12 ;) $\frac{1}{20}$ of $50 is $2½, and $\frac{9}{20}$ of $50 is 9 times $2½, equal to $22½. Therefore, &c.*

12. What is the interest of $75.60 for 4 years 5 months and 10 days, at 9 per cent. ?

13. What is the interest of $50 for 6 years 4 months and 24 days, at 5 per cent. ?

14. What is the interest of $300 for 4 years 7 months and 15 days, at 8 per cent. ?

15. What is the interest of $288 for 8 months 10 days, at 7½ per cent. ?

16. What is the interest of $1200 for 20 days, at 6 per cent. ?

17. What is the interest of $40 for 9 months 5 days, at 4½ per cent. ?

18. What is the interest of $36.72 for 5 years 6 months and 20 days, at 7 per cent. ?

19. What is the interest of $120 for 2 years 1 month and 6 days, at 12⅓ per cent. ?

20. What is the interest of $24 for 11 months and 20 days, at 15 per cent. ?

21. What is the interest of $2000 for 18 days, at 5 per cent. ?

22. What is the interest of $1500 for 2 months and 24 days, at 6 per cent. ?

90. 1. What will be the amount of $60 for 2 years 6 months, at 6 per cent. ?

ANALYSIS. *Since the interest is equal to $\frac{3}{20}$ of the principal, (88,) and the amount is equal to the principal and interest, it follows that $\frac{20}{20}$, the principal, added to $\frac{3}{20}$, the interest, equals $\frac{23}{20}$, the amount.* $\frac{1}{20}$ *of $60 is $3, and $\frac{23}{20}$ of $60 is 23 times $3, or $69, the amount. Therefore, &c.*

NOTE. When more convenient, the interest may first be found, to which add the principal, and the result will be the amount.

2. What is the amount of $36 for 4 years 2 months, at 7 per cent. ?

3. What will $120 amount to in 2 years 11 months, at 8 per cent. ?

4. What will $96.48 amount to in 3 years 4 months, at 6¼ per cent. ?

5. What will $80.50 amount to in 6 years 8 months, at 4½ per cent. ?

6. What will $20.25 amount to in 12 years, at 5 per cent. ?

7. What will $1500 amount to in 10 months, at 10 per cent. ?

8. What will $150 amount to in 6 months and 20 days, at 6 per cent. ?

9. What will $250 amount to in 9 months and 18 days, at 7½ per cent. ?

10. What is the amount of $480 for 1 year 10 months and 25 days, at 5 per cent. ?

11. What is the amount of $500 for 3 years 4 months and 24 days, at 6 per cent. ?

12. What is the amount of $240 for 2 years 7 months and 6 days, at 7 per cent. ?

13. What is the amount of $1000 for 5 years 1 month and 6 days, at 4 per cent. ?

14. What is the amount of $120 for 10 years 6 months and 20 days, at 3 per cent. ?

91. 1. What principal in 3 years 9 months, at 8 per cent., will give $90 interest?

ANALYSIS. *Since the interest for 3 years 9 months, at 8 per cent., is $\frac{3}{10}$ of the principal, (88,) $90 must be $\frac{3}{10}$ of the required principal. Since $90 is $\frac{3}{10}$, $\frac{1}{10}$ is $\frac{1}{3}$ of $90, or $30, and $30 is $\frac{1}{10}$ of 10 times $30, or $300, the principal. Therefore, &c.*

2. What principal, in 1 year 8 months, at 9 per cent., will give $36 interest?

3. What principal in 11 months, at 6 per cent., will give $22 interest?

4. What principal in 7 months 15 days, at 8 per cent., will give $40 interest?

5. A rents a store to B for the yearly rent of $300, which is 12 per cent. of its cost; what did it cost?

6. A gentleman bought 6 horses, for which he paid a sum of money which in 2 years 6 months, at 4 per cent., would have given him $90 interest; what did he pay apiece for the horses?

7. A person deposits $\frac{3}{5}$ of his money in the bank, which brings him an annual income of $1500, at 10 per cent.; the remaining $\frac{2}{5}$ he invests in business which yields him 20 per cent. profit; what are his entire capital and his yearly income?

8. Two persons engaged in trade; A furnished $\frac{5}{8}$ of the capital, and B $\frac{3}{8}$; at the end of 3 years and 4 months they found that they had made a clear profit of $5000, which is $12\frac{1}{2}$ per cent. per annum on the money invested; how much capital did each furnish?

9. A capitalist invested $\frac{3}{5}$ of his money in railroad stock, which depreciated 5 per cent. in value; the remaining $\frac{2}{5}$ he invested in bank stock, which at the end of 1 year had gained $1200, which was 12 per cent. of the investment; what was the whole amount of his capital, and what was his entire loss or gain?

92. 1. What principal will, in 3 years 4 months, at 5 per cent, amount to $700.

ANALYSIS. *Since the interest for 3 years 4 months, at 5 per cent., is $\frac{1}{6}$ of the principal,* (**88**,) *the principal* $\frac{6}{6}$, *added to the interest* $\frac{1}{6}$, *equals the amount* $\frac{7}{6}$; *hence* $700 *is* $\frac{7}{6}$ *of the principal. Since* $700 *is* $\frac{7}{6}$, $\frac{1}{6}$ *is* $\frac{1}{7}$ *of* $700, *or* $100, *and* $100 *is* $\frac{1}{6}$ *of* 6 *times* $100, *or* $600. *Therefore, &c.*

2. What principal in 5 years, at 6 per cent., will amount to $1300?

3. What principal in 1 year 6 months, at 8 per cent., will amount to $280?

4. What principal in 4 years 2 months, at 3 per cent., will amount to $630?

5. What principal in 10 years, at 7 per cent., will amount to $340?

6. What principal in 9 months, at 10 per cent., will amount to $172?

7. What principal in 18 months, at 4 per cent., will amount to $530?

8. The amount due on a bond and mortgage is $2900, it having been on interest 7 years 6 months, at 6 per cent.; what was the principal?

9. Two men bought 200 acres of land, and at the end of 2 years sold it for $1500, which was an advance of $12\frac{1}{2}$ per cent. per annum on its cost; what did it cost an acre?

10. A man invested $\frac{2}{3}$ of all he was worth in the lumber trade, and at the end of 2 years 8 months sold out his entire interest for $3100, which was a yearly gain of 9 per cent. on the money invested; how much was he worth when he commenced trade?

11. A's money is to B's as 2 to 3; if $\frac{1}{2}$ of A's money be put at interest for 3 years 9 months, at 10 per cent., it will amount to $550; how much money has each?

93. 1. In what time, at 5 per cent., will $60 gain $15 interest?

ANALYSIS. *The gain, or interest, is $\frac{15}{60}$, or $\frac{1}{4}$ of the principal, equal to 25 per cent. of the principal.* (**77**, Ex. 7.) *If a given principal gain 5 per cent. in 1 year, it will require as many years to gain 25 per cent. as 5 per cent. is contained times in 25 per cent., or 5 years. Therefore, &c.*

Or thus: *Since $60 in 1 year, at 5 per cent., will gain $3 interest, it will require as many years for $60 to gain $15 interest, as $3 is contained times in $15, which is 5 times.*

2. How long will it take $120 to gain $24 interest, at 6 per cent.?

3. In what time will $500 gain $35, at 7 per cent.?

4. In what time will $120 gain $40, at 10 per cent.?

5. In what time will $80 gain $6, at 3 per cent.?

6. In what time will $300 gain $84, at 7 per cent.?

7. In what time will $160 gain $20, at 6¼ per cent.?

8. In what time will $49 gain $12.25, at 5 per cent.?

9. In what time will any given principal double itself at 4 per cent.?

ANALYSIS. *Since, to double itself, any sum of money must gain 100 per cent., at 1 per cent., it will require 100 years, at 4 per cent., $\frac{1}{4}$ of 100 years, or 25 years. Therefore, &c.*

10. In what time will a given principal double itself at 5 per cent.?

11. In what time will a given principal double itself at 7 per cent.?

12. In what time will a given principal double it-self at 6 per cent. ?

13. In what time will a given principal double it-self at 10 per cent. ?

14. -In what time will $500 double itself, at 12½ per cent. ?

15. In what time will $175 double itself at 20 per cent. ?

16. In what time will a given principal treble it-self at 5 per cent. ?

ANALYSIS. *A given principal will treble itself at 1 per cent. in 200 years; at 5 per cent. in ⅕ of 200 years, or 40 years.*

17. In what time will $100 treble itself at 6 per cent. ? at 7 per cent. ? at 8 per cent. ? at 10 per cent. ?

---

94. 1. A man loaned $75 for 4 years, and re-ceived $18 interest ; what was the rate per cent. ?

ANALYSIS. *Since the gain, or interest, for 4 years, is ¹⁸⁄₇₅, or ⁶⁄₂₅ of the principal, for 1 year it is ¼ of ⁶⁄₂₅, or ⁶⁄₁₀₀ of the principal, equal to 6 per cent. Therefore, &c.*
Or, thus : *At 1 per cent., the interest of $1 for 4 years is 4 cents, and of $75 it is 75 times 4 cents, which are 300 cents, equal to $3. Since $3 interest is 1 per cent. of $75 for 4 years, $18 interest is as many per cent. as $3 is contained times in $18, which is 6 times, equal to 6 per cent.*

2. At what per cent. will $200 gain $49 interest in 3½ years ?

3. At what per cent. will $60 gain $25 interest in 4⅙ years ?

4. At what per cent. will $90 gain $27 in 6 years ?

5. At what per cent. will $12 gain $5 in 10 years?

6. At what per cent. will $400 gain $55 interest in 2½ years?

7. At what per cent. will $150 gain $44 interest in 3⅔ years?

8. At what per cent. will $125 gain $37.50 interest in 5 years?

9. At what per cent. will $800 gain $75 interest in 1 year and 3 months?

10. At what per cent. will $180 gain $45 interest in 3 years and 9 months?

11. At what per cent. will $1250 gain $312.50 interest in 2 years 6 months?

12. At what per cent. will $2500 gain $200 interest in 1 year and 4 months?

13. At what per cent. will a given principal double itself in 5 years?

ANALYSIS. *Since a given principal must gain* 100 *per cent. to double itself in* 1 *year, to double itself in* 5 *years will require* ⅕ *of* 100 *per cent., or* 20 *per cent. Therefore, &c.*

14. At what per cent. will a given principal double itself in 10 years?

15. At what per cent. will a given principal double itself in 12 years 6 months?

16. At what per cent. will $200 double itself in 4 years?

17. At what per cent. will $100 double itself in 8 years?

18. At what per cent. will $150 double itself in 15 years?

19. At what per cent. will $500 double itself in 16 years 8 months?

20. At what per cent. will $175 double itself in 2 years 6 months?

95. The *present worth* of a note payable at a future time is such a sum as, put at interest at the given rate per cent. until it becomes due, will amount to the face of the note.

Discount is an allowance made for the payment of money before it becomes due, and is obtained by subtracting the *present worth* from the *given sum* or *face of the note.*

1. What is the present worth of $180 payable in 3 years 4 months at 6 per cent.?

ANALYSIS. *Since the interest for* 3 *years* 4 *months at* 6 *per cent. is* $\frac{1}{5}$ *of the principal,* (**88**,) *the amount,* $180, *is equal to the principal,* $\frac{5}{5}$, *added to the interest,* $\frac{1}{5}$, *equal to* $\frac{6}{5}$ *of the principal. Since* $180 *is* $\frac{6}{5}$ *of the principal,* $\frac{1}{6}$ *of* $180, *or* $30, *is* $\frac{1}{5}$, *and* $30 *is* $\frac{1}{5}$ *of* 5 *times* $30, *or* $150. *Therefore, &c.*

NOTE. The *discount* is the *difference* between $180 and $150, which is $30.

2. What is the present worth of a note for $36.90, payable in 2 years 6 months, at 5 per cent.?

3. What is the present value of a note for $54, due in 5 years, and bearing interest at 7 per cent.?

4. What is the present value of a debt of $124.40, due in 4 years 2 months, at 8 per cent. interest?

5. What is the discount of $2100, due in 1 year 3 months, at 4 per cent.?

6. What is the discount on a note of $560, payable in 2 years, at 6 per cent. interest?

7. What is the difference between the interest and the discount of $130, due 10 months hence, at 10 per cent.?

8. A man, having a span of horses for sale, offered them for $480 cash in hand, or a note of $550 due in 1 year 8 months without interest. The buyer accepted the latter offer; did the seller gain or lose by his offer, and how much, allowing the money to be worth 6 per cent.?

96. 1. B sold a horse for $\frac{3}{4}$ of $1\frac{3}{5}$ times the cost; what was the gain per cent.?

2. A cow purchased for $28 in the spring was sold for $21 in autumn; what was the loss per cent.?

3. An old lady bought 30 apples of John at the rate of 2 for a cent, as many more of William at the rate of 3 for a cent, and sold the whole at the rate of 5 for 2 cents; did she gain or lose, and at what rate per cent.?

4. Did she gain or lose on the purchase made of John or William, and at what rate per cent. on the amount of the purchase?

5. A hogshead of molasses was bought for $20; $11\frac{1}{8}$ per cent. of it leaked out; how must the remainder be sold per gallon to gain 40 per cent. on the cost?

6. A manufacturer sold 2 machines for $391 each; on one he gained 15 per cent., on the other he lost 15 per cent.; did he gain or lose on the sale of both, and how much?

7. How much wheat must be taken to mill, that 6 bushels may be retained after giving toll of 6 pounds per bushel, or 10 per cent. for grinding?

8. A man brought home 1500 feet of lumber after giving $37\frac{1}{2}$ per cent. of the whole for sawing; how much lumber did he have sawed?

9. A farmer sold 2 horses for $150 apiece; on one he gained 25 per cent., on the other he lost 25 per cent.; did he gain or lose on both, and how much?

10. For hulling barley, 36 per cent. is taken for pay; at this rate, how many bushels must be taken that 32 bushels be returned after hulling?

11. In a school district $57 was to be collected for teacher's wages; the collector was to have 5 per cent. on all moneys collected; how much must he collect to pay his fee and the teacher?

12. Ho.; much plaster must A have ground, to bring home 14 tons, after the miller has taken $12\frac{1}{2}$ per cent. of all he has ground?

13. In how many years, at 5 per cent., will a given principal amount to the same as it would at 7 per cent. in 3 years?

14. At what rate per cent. in 12 years will a given principal amount to the same as at 7 per cent. for 8 years?

15. A farm rents for $500 a year, which is $6\frac{1}{4}$ per cent. on the purchase money, at $40 per acre; how many acres in the farm?

16. Mr. Jones paid $44 interest on a note running 4 years 4 months and 24 days, at 5 per cent.; what was the face of the note?

17. A's note of $200 was given for a carriage; 5 years 7 months and 6 days afterwards, $256 was given for the note; what rate per cent. was paid?

18. A note of $300 on interest at 6 per cent. was given for a span of horses; when the note was taken up, $330 was paid for it; how long did it run?

19. B, on being asked how much he owed for his farm, replied, "I pay 9 per cent. on the debt; if I paid but 7 per cent., it would be $60 in my favor yearly." What did he owe?

20. If Aaron had purchased his horses for 5 per cent. less than he did, they would have cost him $190; how much did he pay for them?

21. If I had purchased my farm for 6 per cent. less than I paid for it, it would have made a difference in the purchase money of $120; what did the farm cost me?

22. A speculator sold wheat for 90 cents a bushel, and in so doing lost 10 per cent.; what should he have sold it for, to have gained 15 per cent.?

23. A nurseryman sold apple trees at $15 per

thousand, and cleared $\frac{2}{5}$ of his receipts; what per cent. profit did he make?

24. B pays $400 a year for the use of 100 acres of land, giving 8 per cent. of its value; what is it worth per acre?

25. I bought a stock of goods for $800, and paid $15 for store rent, $35 for clerk hire, and sold them at the end of 6 months; what per cent. must be made on the goods to cover expenses?

26. In how many years will a man, paying interest at 7 per cent. on a debt for land, pay the amount of the debt in interest?

27. A. bought a farm for $3000; he realized $700 from the sale of wheat, $200 from corn and barley, and $100 from fruit, and then sold the farm at a discount of 25 per cent.; did he gain or lose, and how much?

28. B bought a horse for $60, then sold him for $100, and repurchased him for $80; what was the gain per cent. on the original investment?

29. A milkman sold milk for 4 cents a quart, by which he cleared $\frac{1}{4}$ of the receipts; but milk becoming scarce, he sold for 5 cents; what per cent. did he make at the latter price?

30. A walked 5 per cent. of a journey of 300 miles; 20 per cent. of the remainder he rode in the stage, and the rest of the way in the cars; how far did he ride in the cars?

31. A mechanic sold a buggy for $54, and gained 20 per cent.; he then sold another for $54, and lost 10 per cent.; did he gain or lose, and how much?

32. A dealer sold a melodeon for $190, and lost 5 per cent. on it; he then sold another for the same money, but made enough to balance the loss on the first; what per cent. did he make on the second?

CHAPTER IX.

MISCELLANEOUS EXAMPLES.

97. 1. A gentleman, owning $\frac{4}{5}$ of a vessel, sold $\frac{3}{4}$ of his share; what part of the vessel does he still own?

ANALYSIS. *Since he sold $\frac{3}{4}$ of his share, he would have $\frac{1}{4}$ left, and $\frac{1}{4}$ of $\frac{4}{5}$ is $\frac{1}{5}$. Therefore, &c.*

2. A man, owning $\frac{7}{9}$ of a share in the Central Railroad, sold $\frac{6}{7}$ of it; what part of a share has he left?

3. A man, having $\frac{1}{2}$ of a barrel of flour, gave $\frac{1}{3}$ of it to a poor neighbor; what part of a barrel has he left?

4. Harry, having $\frac{2}{3}$ of a dollar, gave $\frac{3}{5}$ of it for a knife; what part of a dollar has he left?

5. A man sold a watch for $18, which was $\frac{3}{4}$ of what it cost him; how much did he lose?

6. A grocer sold a quantity of cheese for $45, which was $\frac{9}{8}$ of what it cost him; how much did he gain?

7. A threshing machine was sold for $120, at a sacrifice of $\frac{2}{3}$ of the cost; what was the loss on it?

8. Henry having lost $\frac{3}{4}$ of his money playing cards, lent $\frac{1}{4}$ of the remainder, when he found he had $22 left; how much had he at first?

9. A horse was sold for $80, which was $\frac{1}{2}$ of $\frac{2}{3}$ of twice the cost; what was lost on the horse?

10. A man bought a wagon for $54, which was $\frac{3}{7}$ of twice as much as he sold it for; what did he gain?

11. Homer had 15 marbles, which was $\frac{5}{8}$ of 3 times as many as Henry had; how many had Henry?

12. Thomas gave 4 cents for a top, which was $\frac{2}{3}$ times $\frac{1}{2}$ of what money he had; how many marbles, at 2 for a cent, could he buy with what he had left?

13. A farmer, after selling $\frac{3}{5}$ of his flock of sheep, had 20 left ; how many had he at first ?

14. A pole was standing $\frac{2}{5}$ of its length in the air, $\frac{2}{3}$ of the remainder in the water, and 3 feet in the mud ; how many feet in the air ?

15. If from my age you take $\frac{1}{5}$ and $\frac{2}{3}$ of my age, the remainder will be 4 years ; how old am I ?

16. If to $\frac{2}{3}$ of the cost of A's coat you add $12, the sum will be $20 ; what was the cost of the coat ?

17. A drover, being asked how many sheep he had, replied, " If to $\frac{1}{5}$ my number you add 80 sheep, the sum will be 5 more than 3 times my number ; " how many had he ?

18. John and James play at marbles ; John wins 16, which is $\frac{2}{3}$ of twice as many as James now has ; when they began, $\frac{3}{5}$ of John's equaled $\frac{3}{7}$ of James's ; how many had each when they began ?

19. $\frac{3}{4}$ of Herbert's age, increased by 10 years, equals $1\frac{1}{4}$ times his age ; how old is he ?

20. A cow-cost $40 ; $\frac{2}{5}$ of this sum was $\frac{2}{11}$ of $2\frac{2}{3}$ times $\frac{1}{4}$ of the cost of a horse ; what was the cost of the horse ?

21. A. was 25 years of age when he was married, and his age was $\frac{5}{7}$ times $\frac{1}{4}$ of his wife's age ; how old was she ?

22. A post-office was robbed by a clerk, who took $\frac{4}{5}$ of the money in the drawer ; when he was arrested, he had made away with $\frac{3}{4}$ of it, and had $10 left ; how much was in the drawer at first ?

23. A's farm cost $1500 ; $\frac{2}{3}$ of this is $\frac{5}{8}$ of 4 times the cost of the barn ; what did the barn cost ?

24. At the battle of Long Island, the Americans lost 500 men ; $\frac{3}{5}$ of this number was $\frac{2}{3}$ of $\frac{3}{100}$ of their force ; how many men had they in the field ?

25. At Ridgefield, 100 Americans were killed ; $\frac{2}{5}$ of the slain was $7\frac{1}{2}$ times $\frac{1}{100}$ of the men on duty ; how many on duty ?

26. The American loss at the battle of Trenton, in killed, frozen, and wounded, was 60 men ; $\frac{5}{6}$ of this number was $2\frac{1}{2}$ times $\frac{1}{150}$ of the number engaged ; how many men in the engagement ?

27. At the assault on Quebec, the Americans had 100 killed ; $\frac{4}{5}$ of this number was 6 more than $1\frac{3}{4}$ times $\frac{1}{20}$ of the men sent; how many men were in the detachment ?

28. The American loss in the battle of Port Royal Island was 30 men ; $2\frac{1}{3}$ times this number was $3\frac{1}{3}$ times $\frac{1}{10}$ of the number in the field ; how many in the field ?

29. At Germantown, the American loss, in slain, wounded, and prisoners, was 1200 ; $\frac{5}{6}$ of this number was $8\frac{1}{3}$ times $\frac{1}{100}$ of $\frac{1}{5}$ of the army, lacking 1000 men ; how many in the army ?

---

98. 1. Divide 28 into two numbers that shall be to each other as 5 to 2.

ANALYSIS. *Since the numbers are to each other as 5 to 2, the given sum must be divided into 7 equal parts, and 5 of those parts will equal one of the numbers, and 2 of them the other ; the numbers will be $\frac{5}{7}$ of 28 and $\frac{2}{7}$ of 28, equal to 20 and 8. Therefore, &c.*

2. Two men bought 40 bushels of potatoes ; one paid $6, and the other $4 ; how many bushels should each have ?

3. Two travelers, 49 miles apart, approach each other ; one travels 4 miles an hour, the other 3 miles an hour ; how many miles will each travel ?

4. A and B hired a horse and buggy for $25 ; A used it 3 weeks, B 2 weeks ; what should each pay ?

5. Two men hired a pasture for $24 ; one put in 5 cows, the other put in 3 cows ; what should each pay ?

6. Two men hired a field for $12; one put in 2 horses for 2 weeks, the other two horses for 4 weeks; what should each pay?

7. John had 9 cents, and Jay had 7; they gave them all for 32 figs; how many should each of them have?

8. A and B enter into partnership; A invests $10 for 5 months, B invests $5 for 8 months; they gain $45; what is each man's share of the gain?

9. A, B, and C bought a horse; A paid $5 as often as B $4 and C $3; they gained $24 in selling him; what is each man's share of the gain?

10. Three men agree to mow a field for $40; A sends 2 men three days, B sends 3 men three days, C sends 2 men two and a half days; what should each receive?

11. A, B, and C traded in company; A put in $30, B $50, and C such a sum that he took $10 of the $42 gained during the year; what was the gain of A and B, and what C's stock?

12. An ignorant partner, who furnished $500 of a capital of $800, on which $240 had been gained, took $145 for his share of the profits; did he gain or lose, and how much?

13. Two men paid $11 for the use of a pasture; the first put in 5 calves, the second 4 colts; what should each pay, provided 2 colts consume as much as 3 calves?

14. A, B, and C hire a field for $42; A puts in 5 cows, B 3 cows, and C pays $\frac{1}{3}$ of the rent; how much must A and B pay, and how many cows does C put in?

15. Three men paid $56 for a pasture; the first put in 9 oxen, the second 8 cows, and the third 10 calves; what should each pay, if 4 cows eat as much as 3 oxen, and 5 calves as much as 4 cows?

16. Mary and Melissa wrote 60 lines in a copy book; Mary wrote $\frac{1}{8}$ as many lines as Melissa; how many lines did each write?

17. A gardener gave 24 pears to some school children, giving each girl 4 pears, and each boy 3; the boys received as many pears as the girls; how many children were there?

18. A father divided $96 among his two sons and 3 daughters, giving each son $\frac{1}{2}$ as much as each daughter; how much did each receive?

---

99. 1. Three boys have 76 marbles; the second has 2 more than the first, and the third has 6 more than the second; how many has each?

2. James, Henry, and Joseph, together, have 72 apples; Henry has 2 more than James, and Joseph 2 more than Henry; if each had no more than James, how many would all have?

3. If each had as many as Joseph, how many would all have?

4. How many must Joseph give James that each may have the same number? How many has each?

5. A, B, and C built a warehouse for $600; B paid $100 more than A, and C paid as much as A and B; how much did each pay?

6. William bought a rifle, a watch, and a drum, for $42; for the rifle he gave twice as much as for the drum, and for the watch twice as much as for the rifle; what did he give for each?

7. A span of horses, wagon, and harness cost $225; the difference between the cost of the horses and wagon was $1\frac{1}{2}$ times the cost of the harness, and the cost of the horses was 4 times the cost of the harness; what was the cost of each?

8. B traveled 114 miles in 3 days; the first day

he traveled $\frac{1}{2}$ as far as on the last 2 days, and the last day $\frac{1}{2}$ as far as on the first two days; how far did he travel each day?

9. A laborer in one week dug 5 rods more than $\frac{1}{2}$ the length of a ditch, and the next week he dug the remaining 20 rods; how long was the ditch?

ANALYSIS. *Since he dug 5 rods more than $\frac{1}{2}$ of the ditch the first week, the remainder, 20 rods, increased by 5 rods, must equal $\frac{1}{2}$ the ditch; 20 rods + 5 rods = 25 rods, which is $\frac{1}{2}$ of twice 25, or 50 rods. Therefore, &c.*

10. A farmer, owing a store debt, paid at one time $10 more than $\frac{1}{2}$ of it, at another $20 more than $\frac{1}{2}$ of the remainder, and gave a note of $20 for the balance of the debt; what was the amount of the debt?

11. Arthur gave 2 more than $\frac{1}{3}$ of his pennies for a top, 1 more than $\frac{1}{2}$ of the remainder for a whip, and had 4 left; how many pennies had he at first?

12. A grocer, selling beer, drew $\frac{1}{2}$ a gallon more than $\frac{1}{2}$ the contents of a keg one day, the next day he drew $\frac{1}{2}$ a gallon more than $\frac{1}{2}$ of the remainder, and the third day, when he went to draw, he found the keg was empty; how many gallons in the keg at first?

13. A and B have $55; $\frac{1}{2}$ of A's money equals $\frac{3}{5}$ of B's; how many dollars has each?

ANALYSIS. *Since $\frac{1}{2}$ of A's money equals $\frac{3}{5}$ of B's, 2 halves, or all of A's, will equal 2 times $\frac{3}{5}$, or $\frac{6}{5}$ of B's; then A has 6, and B 5 equal parts of the money, and both have 11 parts; $\frac{1}{11}$ of $55 is $5, or 1 part; 6 times $5 are $30, or A's share; and 5 times $5 are $25, or B's share. Therefore, &c.*

14. If 34 apples be divided between John and Mary, so that $\frac{2}{3}$ of John's may equal $\frac{3}{4}$ of Mary's, how many will each have?

15. A and B have together 83 sheep; $\frac{2}{3}$ of A's flock, increased by 8 sheep, is equal to B's flock; how many sheep has each?

16. If 10 cents be taken from $\frac{3}{4}$ of Mary's money, the remainder will be equal to Susan's; the girls, together, have 39 cents; how many cents has each?

17. Homer has 3 marbles more than Silas, and $\frac{3}{5}$ of Homer's marbles equal $\frac{6}{7}$ of Silas's: how many has each?

---

100. 1. One man will drink a gallon of beer in 3 days; another will drink a gallon in 4 days; how long will a gallon last both of them?

2. Julia can do the washing in 7 hours; with Jane's assistance she can do it in 4 hours; in what time can Jane do it?

3. Two boys can pitch a quantity of hay in 5 hours; the first can do it in 9 hours; in what time can the second do it?

4. A cistern can be emptied by 2 pipes in $3\frac{5}{8}$ hours, but 1 pipe will empty it in $7\frac{1}{4}$ hours; in how many hours will the other empty it?

5. A can make a vest in $\frac{3}{5}$ of a day, B in $\frac{3}{4}$, and C in $\frac{5}{6}$ of a day; how many more vests can A and B make in a day than C can?

6. Susan can knit a pair of mittens in $\frac{3}{5}$ of a day, and Sarah can knit a pair in $\frac{3}{7}$ of a day; how many pairs can both knit in a day?

7. What part of a day must Sarah assist Susan that Susan may complete 2 pairs?

8. What part of a day must Susan assist Sarah that Sarah may complete 3 pairs?

9. Jason can hoe 10 rows of corn in $\frac{3}{4}$ of an hour, and Jesse can hoe them in $\frac{3}{5}$ of an hour; in what time can both together hoe them?

10. In what time can Jason hoe what remains after Jesse has hoed ½ an hour?

11. In what time can Jesse hoe what remains after Jason has hoed ⅓ of an hour?

12. How many rows can both hoe in 1 hour?

13. A and B can clear a field in 15 days; with the help of C they can do it in 9 days; in how many days can C do it?

14. A and B can dig a well in 6 days, A and C in 8 days, and B and C in 9 days; in how many days can each dig it, working alone?

15. In how many days can they do it working together?

16. Patrick, Peter, and Philo can dig 40 rods of ditch in 10 days; Patrick and Peter can do it in 15 days; Peter and Philo can do it in 13⅓ days; in how many days can Patrick and Philo dig 28 rods?

17. How long will it take each man to dig 30 rods?

18. Henry and Harlan can cut a field of corn in 6⅔ days; Harlan's day's work exceeds Henry's by ¼ of Henry's; in how many days can each cut the field?

19. Three men can do a piece of work in 10 days; the first does ¾ as much as the second, the third does ⅖ as much as the first and second; in how many days will each do it?

20. In how many days will the first and second do it?

21. In how many days will the first and third do it?

22. In how many days will the second and third do it?

23. A, B, and C can do a piece of work in 8 days; B and C can do it in 12 days, and A and B in 10 days; in how many days can each, working separately, do it?

24. A cistern can be discharged by 3 pipes in 4 hours; the first and second pipes will discharge it in

8 hours ; the first and third in 6 hours ; in what time will each pipe discharge it ?

25. Three men can trench a field in 10 days; A and B can do it in 20 days ; B and C can do it in 15 days; in how many days can A and C trench the same field ?

26. A barrel of flour would last a brother, sister, and servant 30 days; when the brother was absent it would last 60 days; when the sister was absent it would last 45 days; how long would it last the sister after all had used from it 20 days ?

---

101. 1. Benjamin, meeting some beggars, gave each of them 5 cents; had he given them 7 cents apiece, it would have taken 8 cents more ; how many beggars were there ?

ANALYSIS. *Since 2 cents was the increase paid to 1 beggar, and 8 cents the increase paid to all, there were as many beggars as 2 is contained times in 8, which is 4 times. Therefore, &c.*

2. Edward gave 6 plums to each of his playmates, and had 9 remaining ; had he given each of them 8, he would have had but 1 left; how many playmates had he ?

3. Three times a certain number is 15 less than 6 times the same number ? what is the number ?

4. Susan, purchasing calico, found that if she took that at 8 cents a yard she would have 11 cents left; but if she took that at 12 cents a yard she would need 17 cents to pay for it ; how many yards did she want ?

5. 4 times a number is 15 less than $6\frac{1}{2}$ times the same number ; what is the number ?

6. John, being asked how many marbles he had, replied, " $\frac{5}{9}$ of them exceed $\frac{1}{8}$ of them by 4." How many had he ?

7. 5½ times a number is 21 greater than 3⅖ times the same number; what is the number?

8. If 24 chestnuts be divided among some boys, giving 4 apiece to ½ of them, and 2 apiece to the others, how many boys are there?

ANALYSIS. *Since one boy received 4 chestnuts as often as another received 2 chestnuts, 2 boys received 6 chestnuts; there were as many times 2 boys as 6 is contained times in 24, which is 4 times, and 4 times 2 boys are 8 boys. Therefore, &c.*

9. Mary gave her chickens 26 grains of corn; ⅔ of them had 5 grains each, the others but 3 each; how many chickens had she?

NOTE. The above gives the following question : —

10. 5 times ⅔ of a certain number, plus 3 times ⅓ of the same number, is 26; what is the number?

11. A class received 29 merit marks; ⅓ of them received 5 apiece, ½ of the remainder 3 apiece, ⅔ of the remainder 2 apiece, and the rest 1 apiece; how many scholars in the class?

12. 26 melons were stolen, ½ of the party getting 4 each, the rest 3 apiece, except 2, who obtained but 2 apiece; how many were there in the party?

ANALYSIS. *Had the last 2 obtained 3 each, there would have been 28 melons; then 4 times ½ of a number, plus 3 times ½ of the same number, or ⁷⁄₂, would equal 28. Since 28 is ⁷⁄₂ of a number, ⅐ of 28, or 4, is ½, and 4 is ½ of 2 times 4, or 8. Therefore, &c.*

13. 4 times ½ of a number, plus 3½ times the same number, is equal to 28 plus 5; what is the number?

14. Henry said that 4 years more than ⅓ of his age, increased by 5 times ⅓ of it, and that sum by 4 times ⅓ of his age less 4, would make the sum 50 years; how old was he?

15. A drover paid \$5 a head for $\frac{1}{3}$ of his flock, \$4 a head for as many more, \$3 a head for $\frac{1}{2}$ of the remainder, and \$2 a head for the rest; the flock cost \$115; how many sheep had he?

16. A grocer received \$10 for a lot of baskets; for $\frac{1}{4}$ of them he had 6 dimes each, for $\frac{1}{2}$ of the remainder plus 3, 4 dimes each, for $\frac{1}{3}$ of the rest plus 2, 3 dimes each, and for the rest 2 dimes each; how many baskets did he sell?

17. 5 times Henry's age is 3 more than 4 times $\frac{2}{3}$ of it increased by 6 times $\frac{1}{3}$ of it; how old is he?

ANALYSIS. 5 *times Henry's age equals* $\frac{15}{3}$, 4 *times* $\frac{2}{3}$ *of it, plus* 6 *times* $\frac{1}{3}$ *of it, equals* $\frac{14}{3}$, *and* $\frac{15}{3}$ *less* $\frac{14}{3}$ *equals* $\frac{1}{3}$ *of it, which, according to the conditions of the question, is* 3; *and* 3 *is* $\frac{1}{3}$ *of* 3 *times* 3, *or* 9. *Therefore, &c.*

18. 6 times a number is 4 less than 7 times $\frac{3}{4}$ of it, plus 5 times $\frac{1}{4}$ of the same number; what is the number?

19. Bridget, wishing to get a certain number of pounds of meat, found, if she took beef at 5 cents, she would have 4 cents left; if pork at 7 cents, she had not money enough to pay for it; and therefore she took $\frac{3}{4}$ of the quantity in beef, the rest in pork, and paid for it; how many pounds did she get?

20. Four times a number is 6 greater than 5 times $\frac{5}{7}$ of the same number; what is the number?

21. A farmer, wishing to buy a flock of sheep, found, if he paid \$2 a head, he would have \$60 left; if he paid \$5 a head, he had not enough to pay for them; if he took $\frac{1}{2}$ the number at each price, he could just pay for them; how many sheep would his money buy?

22. Twice $\frac{3}{4}$ of a number equals the number plus 8; what is the number?

102. 1. The sum of two numbers is 27; their difference 5; what are the numbers?

ANALYSIS. *Since 27 is the sum of two numbers whose difference is 5, 27 less 5, or 22, would be twice the less number; ½ of 22 is 11, the less number, which increased by 5 equals 16, or the greater number. Therefore, &c.*

2. James and John together have 19 peaches; John has 3 more than James; how many has each?

3. Hobart has 9 marbles more than Herbert, and together they have 31; how many has each?

4. Two men are 37½ miles apart, and travel toward each other; when they meet, one has traveled 5½ miles more than the other; how far has each traveled?

5. Horace, finding he had 5 more apples than Homer, gave him 3, when they together had 21; how many had each then?

6. Mary has twice as many berries as Martha, and together they have 12 quarts; how many quarts has each?

7. A farmer had 47 sheep in two fields; in one field there were 5 more than twice as many as in the other; how many were there in each field?

8. There are 54 bushels of corn in two bins; in one bin there are 6 bushels less than half as many as there are in the other; how many bushels in each?

9. A man bought a watch and chain for $96; the watch cost $4 less than 3 times the cost of the chain; what was the cost of each?

10. Hiram and Harvey built wall 11 days; Hiram received 2 dimes a day more than Harvey, and they both received $25.30; what did each receive, and how much per day?

11. The sum of A's and B's ages is 60 years; 6 years ago, A's age was ⅓ of B's; what are their ages now?

12. A horse and cow cost $124; the horse cost $4 more than 3 times the cost of the cow; what was the cost of each?

13. A farmer paid $24 for a colt and cow; $\frac{1}{2}$ the cost of the colt, multiplied by $\frac{1}{4}$ the cost of the cow, equaled the cost of the cow; what did he pay for each?

14. A lady purchased a dish and cover for 24 dimes; $\frac{1}{6}$ of the cost of the dish, increased by the difference between the cost of the dish and cover, equals the cost of the cover; what was the cost of each?

15. A grocer purchased 25 pounds of butter of two women; $\frac{1}{8}$ of the number of pounds he took of one, increased by the difference between the amounts purchased of both, equals the number of pounds he took of the other; how many pounds did each sell?

16. The sum of two numbers is 10; their difference is equal to $\frac{1}{3}$ of the greater number; what are the numbers?

17. A wagon cost $38; $\frac{9}{11}$ of the cost of the wood work exceeds the cost of ironing it by $\frac{1}{3}$ of the difference between the expense of the two; what was the cost of each?

18. Emily purchased some lace and some ribbon for 30 cents; $\frac{1}{2}$ the cost of the lace, increased by $\frac{1}{2}$ the difference between the cost of the lace and ribbon, equals the cost of the ribbon; what did she pay for each?

19. Wilber paid 20 shillings for a pair of skates and a knife; twice the difference between the cost of the two, plus $\frac{1}{2}$ the cost of the knife, equals the cost of the skates; what did he pay for each?

20. A horse and harness cost $34; $\frac{3}{4}$ of the cost of the horse is $1 more than the cost of the harness; what was the cost of each?

103.   1. A grocer paid $12.60 for 30 bushels of potatoes, giving 50 cents a bushel for good ones, and 20 cents a bushel for poor ones; how many bushels were good?

ANALYSIS. *If all had been good, he would have paid $15, or $2.40 more than he did; each bushel of poor ones made a difference of 30 cents: hence there were as many bushels of poor ones as 30 cents (the difference on 1 bushel) is contained times in $2.40, (the difference on all,) which is 8 times, equal to 8 bushels of poor ones; the difference between 30 bushels and 8 bushels is 22 bushels, equal to the good ones. Therefore, &c.*

2. A farmer bought 28 sheep for $76, paying $3 for old sheep, and $2 for yearlings; how many old sheep?

3. A flour merchant paid $82 for 20 barrels of flour, giving $4.50 for first quality, and $3.50 for second quality; how many barrels were first quality?

4. Henry sold his watch for $18, and by so doing lost $\frac{3}{5}$ of what it cost; what did it cost?

5. A man, employing an equal number of men and boys, paid each boy 5 dimes, and each man 7 dimes, and to them all he paid $7.20; how many were there of both?

6. An old lady sold an equal number of chickens and turkeys for $4, receiving for chickens 3 dimes each, and for turkeys 5 dimes each; how many fowls did she sell?

7. A speculator bought an equal quantity of wheat and beans, giving $1.50 per bushel for wheat, and $1 for beans; the wheat cost $7 more than the beans; how many bushels of beans did he buy?

8. A man engaged to work 25 days, on condition that he should receive $2 for every day's labor, and

pay $1 for board every day he was idle ; he received at settlement $38 ; how many days was he idle ?

ANALYSIS. *As many days as* $3, (*the difference made by 1 idle day,) is contained times in* $12, (*the difference made by all the idle days,) which is 4 times. Therefore he was idle* 4 *days.*

9. A man was engaged for 20 days to copy, re-ceiving $2.50 for every day's labor, and forfeiting $1 for every day he was idle; he received $43; how many days did he copy?

10. Job, having some chestnuts, gave $\frac{2}{5}$ of them to John, who, after eating 6, gave $\frac{3}{4}$ of what remained to his sister, and still had 5 left; how many had Job?

ANALYSIS. *If John gave* $\frac{3}{4}$ *to his sister, the* 5 *left was* $\frac{1}{4}$; 5 *is* $\frac{1}{4}$ *of* 4 *times* 5, *or* 20, *and* 20, *plus the* 6 *he ate, make* 26, *which is* $\frac{3}{5}$ *of Job's, &c.*

11. Mary gave $\frac{3}{4}$ of her flowers to her playmates, $\frac{3}{4}$ of the remainder to her teacher, and had 2 left; how many had she at first?

12. A farmer sold $\frac{4}{5}$ of $1\frac{1}{8}$ times his flock, and had 12 sheep remaining; how many sheep had he at first?

13. A man paid $5 more than $\frac{3}{4}$ of his grocer's bill ; soon after he paid $\frac{2}{5}$ of what remained unpaid, when he found $3 was still due; what was the amount of his bill?

14. John paid $10 more .than $\frac{1}{2}$ of his year's wages for clothes, $12 for a watch; he then lent $\frac{2}{3}$ of what he had left, and having paid $3 for a pair of boots, had $5 left; what were his wages?

15. A laborer engaged to work 20 days, on con-dition that he should have 12 dimes for a day's labor, and pay 2 dimes for every idle day for board ; he received as many dollars as he worked days; how many days was he idle?

104. 1. A rope 28 feet in length was broken so that $\frac{2}{5}$ of the longer piece was equal to the shorter; what was the length of each piece?

ANALYSIS. *The longer piece is divided into 5 equal parts, 2 of which equal the shorter; the sum of the 2 pieces is 7 equal parts, one of which equals $\frac{1}{7}$ of 28 feet, or 4 feet; 2 parts equal 2 times 4 feet, which are 8 feet, the shorter piece; 5 parts equal 5 times 4 feet, which are 20 feet, the longer piece. Therefore, &c.*

2. A tree 56 feet high was broken in a storm; $\frac{3}{4}$ of the part standing was equal to the part broken off; what was the length of each part?

3. Henry and Horace have 45 marbles; Horace has $\frac{4}{5}$ as many as Henry; how many has each?

4. A grocer, having opened a barrel containing 160 pounds of sugar, took out $\frac{3}{5}$ as much as he left; how many pounds were left in the barrel?

5. A traveler paid 63 cents for his supper and lodging, paying $\frac{4}{5}$ as much for his supper as for his lodging; what did he pay for his supper?

6. A horse and wagon cost $170; the horse cost $1\frac{1}{8}$ times as much as the wagon; what was the cost of each?

7. Henry traveled 140 miles in 2 days; the first day he traveled $1\frac{1}{3}$ times as far as he did the second; how far did he travel each day?

8. From Buffalo to Bergen is 50 miles, from Bergen to Utica is $1\frac{7}{8}$ times as far as from Utica to Schenectady, which is 280 miles from Buffalo; how many miles from Buffalo to Utica?

9. David caught a trout 17 inches long; the tail was $\frac{2}{5}$ as long as the body, and the head was 3 inches long; how long was the tail?

10. Divide 36 into 2 such parts that $1\frac{4}{7}$ times one shall equal the other.

11. Homer and Harlan have 48 apples; $\frac{3}{4}$ of Homer's, plus 6, equal the number Harlan has; how many has each?

ANALYSIS. *Harlan has 6 more than $\frac{3}{4}$ as many as Homer, which makes the sum 48, 6 greater than if he had but $\frac{3}{4}$ as many; Homer's are divided into 4 parts, of which 3 parts plus 6 apples are equal to Harlan's; then 4 parts plus 3 parts, plus 6 apples, equal 48, 7 parts equal 42, and $\frac{1}{7}$ of 42, or 6, equals 1 part. 3 parts plus 6 equal 24, the number Harlan has, and 4 parts equal 24, the number Homer has. Therefore, &c.*

12. Rochester is 52 miles from Geneva, via Victor; $\frac{5}{11}$ of the distance from Geneva to Victor, plus 4 miles, equals the distance from Victor to Rochester; how far is Victor from each place?

13. From the ground to the top of a church steeple is 146 feet; $\frac{3}{4}$ of the height of the steeple above the church, plus 6 feet, is equal to the height of the church; what is the height of the steeple above the church?

14. A jar and cover weigh 18 pounds; $\frac{1}{2}$ of the weight of the cover, increased by 12 pounds, equals the weight of the jar; what is the weight of each?

15. A coat and vest cost $19; $\frac{1}{3}$ of the cost of the coat, plus $3, equals the cost of the vest; what is the cost of each?

16. Wilson has 15 oranges and lemons; $\frac{1}{2}$ of the oranges equals $\frac{1}{3}$ of the lemons; how many of each has he?

ANALYSIS. *Since $\frac{1}{2}$ of the oranges equals $\frac{1}{3}$ of the lemons, $\frac{2}{2}$, or all the oranges, equal $\frac{2}{3}$ of the lemons; we then have the oranges and lemons divided into 5 equal parts, 2 parts of which equal the oranges, and 3 the lemons, &c.*

17. A father gave his 2 sons 50 cents; $\frac{1}{2}$ of George's money was equal to $\frac{3}{4}$ of Abel's; how many cents had each?

18. Andrew has 34 marbles; $\frac{2}{5}$ of the gray ones

equal $\frac{4}{5}$ of the black ones; how many of each kind were there?

19. The sum of two numbers is 62; $\frac{2}{3}$ of one equal $\frac{5}{8}$ of the other; what are the numbers?

20. A purse and contents are valued at 46 shillings; $\frac{3}{4}$ of the value of the purse is equal to $\frac{2}{5}$ of the value of what is in it; what is the purse worth?

21. A person, being asked the time of day, replied, "The time past noon is equal to $\frac{1}{5}$ of the time to midnight." What was the hour?

ANALYSIS. *The time to midnight is divided into 5 equal parts, one of which equals the time past noon; then 5 parts plus 1 part equals 6 parts; and 12 hours, the time from noon to midnight, must be $\frac{5}{6}$ of the time it lacked of being midnight; since 12 is $\frac{5}{6}$, $\frac{1}{6}$, which is $\frac{1}{5}$ of $\frac{5}{6}$, will be $\frac{1}{6}$ of 12 hours, which is 2 hours. Therefore the hour was 2 o'clock, P. M.*

22. What was the time, provided $\frac{2}{3}$ of the time past midnight equaled the time to 10 o'clock, A. M.?

23. $\frac{2}{3}$ of the time from this instant to 5 o'clock, P. M., equals $\frac{3}{4}$ of the time past midnight; what is the time of day?

24. Peter said to John, "$1\frac{3}{4}$ times my age is $1\frac{3}{5}$ times your age, and the sum of our ages is 36 years." What was the age of each?

25. A bin whose capacity was 44 bushels was partly filled with grain; $2\frac{1}{3}$ times what was in it was $2\frac{4}{5}$ times what it would take to fill it; how many more bushels would fill it?

26. A person, inquiring the distance to Cincinnati, was told that $3\frac{3}{7}$ times what it lacked of being 83 miles was $1\frac{3}{5}$ times what it exceeded 39 miles; how far was he from Cincinnati?

27. The number of miles that the distance from Charleston to Columbia exceeds 100 miles equals $1\frac{1}{2}$ times the distance it lacks of being 150 miles: how far is it from Charleston to Columbia?

105. 1. Two pieces of cloth contain 38 yards; $\frac{2}{3}$ of the first piece equals $\frac{2}{5}$ of the second, plus 4 yards; how many yards in each piece?

ANALYSIS. *If $\frac{2}{3}$ equal $\frac{2}{5} + 4$, $\frac{1}{3}$ will equal $\frac{1}{2}$ of $\frac{2}{5} + 4$, which is $\frac{1}{5} + 2$, this is $\frac{1}{5}$ of 3 times $\frac{1}{5} + 2$, or $\frac{3}{5} + 6$; then we have 1 piece equal to $\frac{3}{5}$ the other plus 6 yards, or 1 piece divided into 5 parts, and 3 of these parts plus 6 yards equal the other piece; hence 5 parts plus 3 parts plus 6 yards equal 38 yards, or 8 parts and 6 yards, equal 38 yards; 38 yards minus 6 yards equal 32 yards, or 8 parts, &c.*

2. A lad inquiring his mother's age, his father replied, "$\frac{3}{4}$ of my age is 9 years more than $\frac{6}{7}$ of your mother's, and the sum of our ages is 72 years." How old was his mother?

3. Two men built 38 rods of wall; $\frac{2}{3}$ of what one built, plus 4 rods, is equal to $\frac{4}{5}$ of what the other built; how many rods did each build?

4. Hiram and Richard sheared 67 sheep; $\frac{4}{7}$ of the number Hiram sheared was 4 more than $\frac{4}{5}$ of the number Richard sheared; how many did each shear?

5. What is the time, providing $\frac{2}{3}$ of the time past midnight, plus $1\frac{1}{15}$ hours, equals $\frac{2}{5}$ of the time to midnight?

6. A, being asked his age, replied, "$1\frac{1}{8}$ times what I lack of being a hundred years old is 9 years more than $1\frac{1}{2}$ times what my age exceeds 64." What was his age?

7. A rope was cut into 3 pieces; the first piece was 5 feet long, the second was as long as the first plus $\frac{1}{2}$ of the third, and the third was as long as the other two; what was the length of the rope?

ANALYSIS. *Since the third piece is as long as the other two, it must be $\frac{1}{2}$ of the rope; the second piece, being $\frac{1}{2}$ as long, is $\frac{1}{4}$; and the 5 feet which the second exceeds $\frac{1}{4}$, with the 5 feet of the first piece, make 10 feet, which must be the other fourth; 4 times 10 is 40. Therefore, &c.*

8. The head of a fish is 7 inches long, the tail is as long as the head and $\frac{1}{2}$ of the body, and the body is as long as the head and tail; what is the length of the fish?

9. A piece of steel was broken into 3 pieces; the first piece was $\frac{1}{5}$ of the whole, the second weighed 3 pounds, and the third weighed as much as the other two; what was the weight of the whole?

10. Three men dig potatoes; the first digs $\frac{1}{3}$ of the whole, lacking 2 bushels, the second digs 5 bushels, and the third digs as many as the other two; how many bushels did all dig?

11. From Batavia to Avon is 24 miles; this distance, plus the distance from Bath to Corning, and 12 miles more, equals the distance from Avon to Bath; from Bath to Corning is $\frac{1}{5}$ of the whole distance; how far from Batavia to Corning?

12. A farmer took money for stock, as follows: $18 for swine, $6 more than $\frac{1}{3}$ of the whole for sheep, and for cattle $7 less than $\frac{3}{8}$ as much as for sheep and swine; how many dollars did he receive?

13. A third and $\frac{1}{2}$ a third of 12 is $\frac{3}{8}$ of twice what number?

14. Stephen spent $\frac{2}{3}$ of his money, and afterward earned $\frac{3}{4}$ as much as he had spent, when he had $16.50 less than at first; how much had he at first?

15. If $\frac{2}{3}$ of a ton of hay cost $\frac{4}{5}$ of an eagle, how many dollars will $\frac{1}{6}$ of a ton cost?

16. A is 6 years more than $\frac{1}{2}$ as old as B, C is $\frac{2}{3}$ as old as A, and B's age is equal to the sum of A's and C's; what is the age of each?

17. A owns 12 more than $\frac{3}{4}$ as many acres as B, C owns $\frac{1}{2}$ as many as A, and B owns 24 acres less than A and C; how many acres has each.

106. 1. Malcom is 8 years old, and Martin 25; in how many years will Malcom be $\frac{1}{2}$ as old as Martin?

ANALYSIS. *8 years since, Martin was 17 years of age; in 17 years from that time, or, since Malcom is 8 years old, in 17 less 8, or 9 years from this time, Malcom will be 17 years old, and Martin will be twice 17, or 34 years old. Therefore, &c.*

2. A father is 22 years older than his son, and the son's age is $\frac{2}{3}$ of the father's; how many years since the son's age was $\frac{1}{2}$ the father's?

3. Helen is 9 years old, her sister is 22; in now many years will Helen be $\frac{1}{2}$ as old as her sister?

4. Henry played at marbles with Charles, who had 45; Henry won as many as he had to commence with; when they quit, each had the same number; how many had both?

ANALYSIS. *Since Henry won as many as he had, he left off playing with twice as many as he began with; and Charles, now having the same number, must have had 3 times as many as Henry when they commenced playing. 45 is 3 times $\frac{1}{3}$ of 45, or 15, and 45 + 15 is 60. Therefore, &c.*

5. A farmer, having 60 sheep in one field, took as many from them as he had in another field, and put them with the others, when the flocks were equal; how many sheep had he?

6. From a bin containing 52 bushels, 2 more than as many bushels as were in another bin were taken and put in the other bin, when both contained the same quantity; how many bushels in both bins?

7. Uncle Simon's age, increased by the difference between $\frac{2}{3}$ and $\frac{1}{4}$ of his age, is 6 more than $\frac{1}{8}$ times his age; how old is he?

8. Henry earned 20 dollars in the spring; in the fall he earned as much as in the spring and $\frac{1}{3}$ as

166   INTELLECTUAL ARITHMETIC.   [**106.**

much as in the summer, and in the summer as much
as in the spring and fall; how much did he earn in
all?

9. A has 10 sheep, C has as many as A and $\frac{2}{3}$ as
many as B, and B has as many as A and C; how
many sheep have they all?

ANALYSIS. *Since B has as many as A and C, he must
have $\frac{1}{2}$ of the whole; then* 10 *sheep, plus* 10 $+$ $\frac{2}{3}$ *of* $\frac{1}{2}$,
plus $\frac{1}{2}$, *equals* $\frac{5}{6}$ $+$ 20, *or the whole number of sheep; hence*
20 *equals* $\frac{1}{6}$ *the number, and* 20 *is* $\frac{1}{6}$ *of* 6 *times* 20, *or* 120
sheep. Therefore, &c.

10. A, owning 74 acres of land, sold B $\frac{3}{4}$ as much
as B owned; then B's farm was $\frac{3}{4}$ as large as A's;
how many acres in each farm?

11. Mary has 10 more chickens than turkeys, yet
$\frac{2}{3}$ of the turkeys equal $\frac{1}{2}$ the chickens; how many
chickens has she?

12. Heman's coat cost $15 less than his whole
suit; $\frac{1}{4}$ of the price of the suit equaled $\frac{2}{3}$ of the price
of the coat; what did the suit cost?

13. Daniel caught 14 pigeons more than his
brother, and $2\frac{2}{3}$ times his brother's equaled $\frac{4}{5}$ of his;
how many did each catch?

14. One number is $3\frac{1}{2}$ times another; if 15 be
added to each, one is just $\frac{1}{2}$ of the other; what are
the numbers?

15. The difference between the cost of a horse
and a buggy is $40; $\frac{4}{5}$ of the cost of the buggy equal
$\frac{8}{15}$ of the cost of the horse; what is the value of
each?

16. Alice is $\frac{1}{3}$ as old as her mother; 5 years since
she was but $\frac{1}{5}$ as old; in how many years will she be
$\frac{1}{2}$ as old?

17. Hobart, having 20 marbles more than Dwight,
plays with him; Dwight wins $\frac{1}{2}$ as many as he had

at first, when Hobart has ⅔ as many left as he commenced with; how many had each at first?

18. The difference between two numbers is 16;
if 4 be taken from the larger and added to the less,
2⅜ times the larger will equal 3⅙ times the smaller;
what are the numbers?

19. Jason bought a watch, and had $20 remain-
ing; he then gave 2 times the cost of the watch for
a rifle, and had ¼ of his money left; what did the
rifle cost?

20. Find the ages of A, B, and C, by knowing
that C's age at A's birth was 5½ times B's, and now
is equal to the sum of A's and B's; also that if A
were now 3 years younger, or B 4 years older, A's
age would be equal to ¾ of B's.

---

107. 1. Two boys are running in the same
direction; one is 27 rods in advance of the other in
pursuit, who gains upon the foremost 3 rods in a
minute; in how many minutes will he be overtaken?

ANALYSIS. *In as many minutes as 3, the number of rods
gained in one minute, is contained times in 27, the number
of rods to be gained.*

2. A, after traveling 2 hours, at the rate of 5
miles an hour, was followed by B, at the rate of 7
miles an hour; in how many hours would B overtake A?

3. A dog in pursuit of a hare which has 28 rods
the start, runs 9 rods while the hare runs 7; how far
will the dog run to catch the hare?

4. Henry saves $5 while John saves $7; how
much will each have when the difference between
what each has saved is $30?

5. A and B started from the same point to run a
race; A ran 84 rods and gave out, when ⅛ of the

distance B had run equaled the distance he was ahead of A; how far did B run?

6. Three men bought a horse; A paid $25, which was $\frac{1}{4}$ of what B and C paid; B paid $\frac{2}{3}$ as much as A and C; what did B and C pay?

7. The hour and minute hands of a watch are together at 12 o'clock; when will they next be to-gether?

ANALYSIS. *Since the minute hand passes the hour hand 11 times in 12 hours, if both are at 12, the minute hand will pass the hour hand the first time in $\frac{1}{11}$ of 12 hours, or in $1\frac{1}{11}$ hours, equal to $5\frac{5}{11}$ minutes past 1 o'clock. There-fore, &c.*

8. A gentleman, being asked the time, replied, "It is between 3 and 4 o'clock, and the hands are directly opposite." What was the time?

9. A fox is 40 leaps ahead of a hound, and takes 7 leaps to the hound's 4; but 3 of the hound's leaps equal 6 of the fox's; how many leaps will the fox take before being caught?

10. A wolf ran 80 rods to catch a sheep; $\frac{3}{5}$ of the distance the sheep ran was equal to the distance be-tween them when the chase commenced; what was the distance?

11. The sum of $\frac{2}{3}$ of A's and $\frac{3}{8}$ of B's money, being on interest 2 years 7 months and 6 days, at 5 per cent., amounted to $2260; $\frac{2}{3}$ of B's money was $1\frac{1}{2}$ times $\frac{2}{5}$ of A's; how much had each?

12. B's fortune is $1\frac{1}{2}$ times A's; the interest of $\frac{1}{2}$ of A's fortune and $\frac{1}{3}$ of B's for 5 years, at 6 per cent., is $600; what is the fortune of each?

13. A drover paid $76 for calves and sheep, pay-ing $3 apiece for calves and $2 for sheep; he sold $\frac{1}{4}$ of his calves and $\frac{2}{5}$ of his sheep for $23, and in so doing lost 8 per cent. on their cost; how many of each did he purchase?

APPENDIX.

THE author desires to call the attention of teachers to the number and variety of *changes* that may be wrought upon the examples of the Sections from which the following have been selected, as well as upon many others of the same class, and which may appropriately be termed " Ringing the Changes." It is not recommended that these changes be applied to all the examples, but used as an occasional exercise, and limited according to the time and convenience of the teacher.

It is recommended to teachers to exercise their classes in these " changes," not so much for the novelty of them, as for the enlivening effect produced upon the class, and *especially* for the peculiar facilities they afford for *thorough mental discipline ;* and while, at first, to some they may appear severe and too mathematical, they will very soon become easy and comprehensible.

To aid beginners, the blackboard may be used to advantage ; and to illustrate, take the example which has been written out in full in Section 71, page 171–3 : —

$$\tfrac{4}{7} \text{ of } 35 \text{ is } \tfrac{5}{8} \text{ of how many thirds of } 18 ?$$

which may be written on the board thus : —

$$\tfrac{4}{7} \times 35 = \tfrac{5}{8} \times {}_{\overline{3}} \times 18 ?$$

Call upon some pupil to read the question according to the *first* form, and to solve the question according to the form of analysis given ; and the answer, if correct, placed over the 3, will fulfill the conditions of the question ; substitute this number, and erase another, thus : —

$$\tfrac{4}{7} \times 35 = \tfrac{5}{8} \times \tfrac{6}{3} \times \text{——} ?$$

which is read

$$\tfrac{4}{7} \text{ of } 35 \text{ is } \tfrac{5}{8} \text{ of } \tfrac{6}{3} \text{ of what number} ?$$

Solve this as before, and so continue until all the numbers have been erased, and replaced by solution.

When the class have become familiar with the exercise, the use of the blackboard should be dispensed with, and the pupil be required to " ring the changes " by simply hearing the first form of the question read.

Each question, and its *form* of solution, should be given by the pupil, but he may be allowed to give *results* in the *solution* that have been *previously* determined by analysis, in order to shorten the work and avoid monotonous repetition.

Members of the class should be called upon promiscuously, and encouraged to ask questions, and to detect errors either in the statement or solution of questions. The teacher should read an example *once*, slowly and distinctly, then call upon some one of the class who shall commence operations, and continue to give questions, forms, solutions, and conclusions, until signaled to sit, or another pupil detecting an error, raises the hand, when some other one should be called upon, who should resume where the last one left off ; and so on.

A teacher who has not practiced a class upon these changes, cannot conceive of the interest, close attention, and perfect enthusiasm that may be created, as well as the thorough mental discipline attained, by this exercise ; and it is firmly believed that, upon trial, it will commend itself to the judgment and approval of every *live* teacher.

12

67. 1. 24 is $\frac{4}{5}$ of how many times 10 ?

24 is $\frac{4}{5}$ of as many times 10 as 10 is contained times in 5 times $\frac{1}{4}$ of 24 ; $\frac{1}{4}$ of 24 is 6, and 5 times 6 is 30; 10 is contained in 30, 3 times. Therefore 24 is $\frac{4}{5}$ of 3 times 10.

2. 24 is $\frac{4}{5}$ of 3 times what number ?

24 is $\frac{4}{5}$ of 3 times $\frac{1}{3}$ of 5 times $\frac{1}{4}$ of 24 ; $\frac{1}{4}$ of 24 is 6, and 5 times 6 is 30 ; $\frac{1}{3}$ of 30 is 10. Therefore 24 is $\frac{4}{5}$ of 3 times 10.

3. 24 is how many fifths of 3 times 10 ?

24 is as many fifths of 3 times 10 as $\frac{1}{5}$ of 3 times 10 is contained times in 24. 3 times 10 is 30, and $\frac{1}{5}$ of 30 is 6, and 6 is contained in 24, 4 times. Therefore 24 is $\frac{4}{5}$ of 3 times 10.

4. 24 is 4 times what part of 3 times 10 ?

24 is 4 times such a part of 3 times 10 as 3 times 10 is contained times in $\frac{1}{4}$ of 24. 3 times 10 is 30, and $\frac{1}{4}$ of 24 is 6 ; 30 is contained in 6, $\frac{6}{30}$ or $\frac{1}{5}$ times. Therefore 24 is 4 times $\frac{1}{5}$, or $\frac{4}{5}$, of 3 times 10.

5. What number is $\frac{4}{5}$ of 3 times 10 ?

4 times $\frac{1}{5}$ of 3 times 10. 3 times 10 is 30, $\frac{1}{5}$ of 30 is 6, and 4 times 6 is 24. Therefore 24 is $\frac{4}{5}$ of 3 times 10.

---

70. 1. $\frac{4}{7}$ of 56 is $\frac{8}{9}$ of 3 times what number ?

$\frac{4}{7}$ of 56 is $\frac{8}{9}$ of 3 times $\frac{1}{3}$ of 9 times $\frac{1}{8}$ of 4 times $\frac{1}{7}$ of 56 ; $\frac{1}{7}$ of 56 is 8, and 4 times 8 is 32 ; $\frac{1}{8}$ of 32 is 4, and 9 times 4 is 36 ; $\frac{1}{3}$ of 36 is 12. Therefore, $\frac{4}{7}$ of 56 is $\frac{8}{9}$ of 3 times 12.

2. $\frac{4}{7}$ of 56 is $\frac{8}{9}$ of how many times 12 ?

$\frac{4}{7}$ of 56 is $\frac{8}{9}$ of as many times 12 as 12 is contained times in 9 times $\frac{1}{8}$ of 4 times $\frac{1}{7}$ of 56 ; $\frac{1}{7}$ of 56 is 8, and 4 times 8 is 32 ; $\frac{1}{8}$ of 32 is 4, and 9 times 4 is 36 ; 12 is contained in 36, 3 times. Therefore $\frac{4}{7}$ of 56 is $\frac{8}{9}$ of 3 times 12.

3. $\frac{4}{7}$ of 56 is how many ninths of 3 times 12 ?

$\frac{4}{7}$ of 56 is as many ninths of 3 times 12 as $\frac{1}{9}$ of 3 times

12 is contained times in 4 times $\frac{1}{7}$ of 56. $\frac{1}{7}$ of 56 is 8, and $\frac{4}{7}$ of 56 is 4 times 8; 4 times 8 is 32; 3 times 12 is 36, $\frac{1}{9}$ of 36 is 4, and 4 is contained in 32, 8 times. Therefore $\frac{4}{7}$ of 56 is $\frac{8}{9}$ of 3 times 12.

4. $\frac{4}{7}$ of 56 is 8 times what part of 3 times 12?

Such a part of 3 times 12 as 3 times 12 is contained times in $\frac{1}{8}$ of 4 times $\frac{1}{7}$ of 56. $\frac{1}{7}$ of 56 is 8, and 4 times 8 is 32; $\frac{1}{8}$ of 32 is 4; 3 times 12 is 36, and 36 is contained in 4, $\frac{4}{36}$ or $\frac{1}{9}$ times. Therefore $\frac{4}{7}$ of 56 is 8 times $\frac{1}{9}$, or $\frac{8}{9}$, of 3 times 12.

5. $\frac{8}{9}$ of 3 times 12 is $\frac{4}{7}$ of what number?

$\frac{8}{9}$ of 3 times 12 is $\frac{4}{7}$ of 7 times $\frac{1}{4}$ of 8 times $\frac{1}{9}$ o. 3 times 12; $\frac{1}{9}$ of 36 is 4, and 8 times 4 is 32; $\frac{1}{4}$ of 32 is 8, and 7 times 8 is 56. Therefore $\frac{8}{9}$ of 3 times 12 is $\frac{4}{7}$ of 56.

6. $\frac{8}{9}$ of 3 times 12 is how many sevenths of 56?

As many sevenths of 56 as $\frac{1}{7}$ of 56 is contained times in 8 times $\frac{1}{9}$ of 3 times 12. 3 times 12 is 36, $\frac{1}{9}$ of 36 is 4, and 8 times 4 is 32; $\frac{1}{7}$ of 56 is 8, and 8 is contained in 32, 4 times. Therefore $\frac{8}{9}$ of 3 times 12 is $\frac{4}{7}$ of 56.

7. $\frac{8}{9}$ of 3 times 12 is 4 times what part of 56?

Such a part of 56 as 56 is contained times in $\frac{1}{4}$ of 8 times $\frac{1}{9}$ of 3 times 12; 3 times 12 is 36; $\frac{1}{9}$ of 36 is 4, and 8 times 4 is 32; $\frac{1}{4}$ of 32 is 8, and 56 is contained in 8, $\frac{8}{56}$ or $\frac{1}{7}$ times. Therefore $\frac{8}{9}$ of 3 times 12 is 4 times $\frac{1}{7}$, or $\frac{4}{7}$, of 56.

---

71. 1. $\frac{4}{7}$ of 35 is $\frac{5}{9}$ of how many thirds of 18?

Expressed by signs on the blackboard thus:—
$$\tfrac{4}{7} \times 35 = \tfrac{5}{9} \times \tfrac{}{3} \times 18?$$
Of as many thirds of 18 as $\frac{1}{3}$ of 18 is contained times in 9 times $\frac{1}{5}$ of 4 times $\frac{1}{7}$ of 35; $\frac{1}{7}$ of 35 is 5, and 4 times 5 is 20; $\frac{1}{5}$ of 20 is 4, and 9 times 4 is 36; $\frac{1}{3}$ of 18 is 6, and 6 is contained in 36, 6 times. Therefore $\frac{4}{7}$ of 35 is $\frac{5}{9}$ of 6 thirds of 18.

2. $\frac{4}{7}$ of 35 is $\frac{5}{9}$ of $\frac{6}{3}$ of what number?
$$\tfrac{4}{7} \times 35 = \tfrac{5}{9} \times \tfrac{6}{3} \times \underline{\quad}?$$
$\frac{4}{7}$ of 35 is $\frac{5}{9}$ of $\frac{6}{3}$ of 3 times $\frac{1}{6}$ of 9 times $\frac{1}{5}$ of 4 times

$\frac{1}{7}$ of 35 ; $\frac{1}{7}$ of 35 is 5, and 4 times 5 is 20 ; $\frac{1}{5}$ of 20 is 4, and 9 times 4 is 36 ; $\frac{1}{6}$ of 36 is 6, and 3 times 6 is 18. Therefore $\frac{4}{7}$ of 35 is $\frac{5}{9}$ of $\frac{6}{3}$ of 18.

3. $\frac{4}{7}$ of 35 is $\frac{5}{9}$ of 6 times what part of 18 ?

$$\tfrac{4}{7}\times 35 = \tfrac{5}{9}\times \tfrac{6}{1}\times 18 ?$$

$\frac{4}{7}$ of 35 is $\frac{5}{9}$ of 6 times such a part of 18 as 18 is contained times in $\frac{1}{6}$ of 9 times $\frac{1}{5}$ of 4 times $\frac{1}{7}$ of 35. $\frac{1}{7}$ of 35 is 5, and 4 times 5 is 20 ; $\frac{1}{5}$ of 20 is 4, and 9 times 4 is 36 ; $\frac{1}{6}$ of 36 is 6, and 18 is contained in 6, $\frac{6}{18}$ or $\frac{1}{3}$ times. Therefore $\frac{4}{7}$ of 35 is $\frac{5}{9}$ of 6 times $\frac{1}{3}$, or $\frac{6}{3}$, of 18.

4. $\frac{4}{7}$ of 35 is how many ninths of $\frac{6}{3}$ of 18 ?

$$\tfrac{4}{7}\times 35 = \tfrac{}{9}\times \tfrac{6}{3}\times 18 ?$$

$\frac{4}{7}$ of 35 is as many *ninths* of $\frac{6}{3}$ of 18 as $\frac{1}{9}$ of 6 times $\frac{1}{3}$ of 18 is contained times in 4 times $\frac{1}{7}$ of 35. $\frac{1}{7}$ of 35 is 5, and 4 times 5 is 20 ; $\frac{1}{3}$ of 18 is 6, and 6 times 6 is 36 ; $\frac{1}{9}$ of 36 is 4, and 4 is contained in 20, 5 times. Therefore $\frac{4}{7}$ of 35 is $\frac{5}{9}$ of $\frac{6}{3}$ of 18.

5. $\frac{4}{7}$ of 35 is 5 times what part of $\frac{6}{3}$ of 18 ?

$$\tfrac{4}{7}\times 35 = \tfrac{5}{}\times \tfrac{6}{3}\times 18 ?$$

$\frac{4}{7}$ of 35 is 5 times such a part of $\frac{6}{3}$ of 18 as 6 times $\frac{1}{3}$ of 18 is contained times in $\frac{1}{5}$ of 4 times $\frac{1}{7}$ of 35. $\frac{1}{7}$ of 35 is 5, and 4 times 5 is 20 ; $\frac{1}{5}$ of 20 is 4 ; $\frac{1}{3}$ of 18 is 6, and 6 times 6, is 36 ; 36 is contained in 4, $\frac{4}{36}$ or $\frac{1}{9}$ times. Therefore $\frac{4}{7}$ of 35 is 5 times $\frac{1}{9}$, or $\frac{5}{9}$, of $\frac{6}{3}$ of 18.

6. $\frac{5}{9}$ of $\frac{6}{3}$ of 18 is $\frac{4}{7}$ of what number ?

$$\tfrac{5}{9}\times \tfrac{6}{3}\times 18 = \tfrac{4}{7}\times \text{------} ?$$

$\frac{5}{9}$ of $\frac{6}{3}$ of 18 is $\frac{4}{7}$ of 7 times $\frac{1}{4}$ of 5 times $\frac{1}{9}$ of 6 times $\frac{1}{3}$ of 18; $\frac{1}{3}$ of 18 is 6, and 6 times 6 is 36 ; $\frac{1}{9}$ of 36 is 4, and 5 times 4 is 20 ; $\frac{1}{4}$ of 20 is 5, and 7 times 5 is 35. Therefore $\frac{5}{9}$ of $\frac{6}{3}$ of 18 is $\frac{4}{7}$ of 35.

7. $\frac{5}{9}$ of $\frac{6}{3}$ of 18 is how many sevenths of 35 ?

$$\tfrac{5}{9}\times \tfrac{6}{3}\times 18 = \tfrac{}{7}\times 35 ?$$

$\frac{5}{9}$ of $\frac{6}{3}$ of 18 is as many *sevenths* of 35 as $\frac{1}{7}$ of 35 is contained times in 5 times $\frac{1}{9}$ of 6 times $\frac{1}{3}$ of 18; $\frac{1}{3}$ of 18 is 6, and 6 times 6 is 36 ; $\frac{1}{9}$ of 36 is 4, and 5 times 4 is 20 ; $\frac{1}{7}$ of 35 is 5, and 5 is contained in 20, 4 times. Therefore $\frac{5}{9}$ of $\frac{6}{3}$ of 18 is $\frac{4}{7}$ of 35.

8. $\frac{5}{9}$ of $\frac{6}{3}$ of 18 is 4 times what part of 35 ?

$$\frac{5}{9} \times \frac{6}{3} \times 18 = \frac{4}{?} \times 35 ?$$

$\frac{5}{9}$ of $\frac{6}{3}$ of 18 is 4 times such a part of 35 as 35 is contained times in $\frac{1}{4}$ of 5 times $\frac{1}{9}$ of 6 times $\frac{1}{3}$ of 18. $\frac{1}{3}$ of 18 is 6, and 6 times 6 is 36 ; $\frac{1}{9}$ of 36 is 4, and 5 times 4 is 20; $\frac{1}{4}$ of 20 is 5, and 35 is contained in 5, $\frac{5}{35}$ or $\frac{1}{7}$ times. Therefore $\frac{5}{9}$ of $\frac{6}{3}$ of 18 is 4 times $\frac{1}{7}$, or $\frac{4}{7}$, of 35.

---

72. 1. $\frac{4}{3}$ of 36 is $\frac{4}{9}$ of how many times $\frac{2}{7}$ of 42 ?

Of as many times $\frac{2}{7}$ of 42 as 2 times $\frac{1}{7}$ of 42 is contained times in 9 times $\frac{1}{4}$ of 4 times $\frac{1}{3}$ of 36 ; $\frac{1}{3}$ of 36 is 12, and 4 times 12 is 48 ; $\frac{1}{4}$ of 48 is 12, and 9 times 12 is 108 ; $\frac{1}{7}$ of 42 is 6, and 2 times 6 is 12, and 12 is contained in 108, 9 times. Therefore $\frac{4}{3}$ of 36 is $\frac{4}{9}$ of 9 times $\frac{2}{7}$ of 42.

2. $\frac{4}{3}$ of 36 is $\frac{4}{9}$ of 9 times $\frac{2}{7}$ of what number ?

$\frac{4}{3}$ of 36 is $\frac{4}{9}$ of 9 times $\frac{2}{7}$ of 7 times $\frac{1}{2}$ of $\frac{1}{9}$ of 9 times $\frac{1}{4}$ of 4 times $\frac{1}{3}$ of 36 ; $\frac{1}{3}$ of 36 is 12, and 4 times 12 is 48 ; $\frac{1}{4}$ of 48 is 12, and 9 times 12 is 108 ; $\frac{1}{9}$ of 108 is 12, $\frac{1}{2}$ of 12 is 6, and 7 times 6 is 42. Therefore $\frac{4}{3}$ of 36 is $\frac{4}{9}$ of 9 times $\frac{2}{7}$ of 42.

3. $\frac{4}{3}$ of 36 is $\frac{4}{9}$ of 9 times how many sevenths of 42 ?

$\frac{4}{3}$ of 36 is $\frac{4}{9}$ of 9 times as many sevenths of 42 as $\frac{1}{7}$ of 42 is contained times in $\frac{1}{9}$ of 9 times $\frac{1}{4}$ of 4 times $\frac{1}{3}$ of 36 ; $\frac{1}{3}$ of 36 is 12, and 4 times 12 is 48 ; $\frac{1}{4}$ of 48 is 12, 9 times 12 is 108 ; $\frac{1}{9}$ of 108 is 12 ; $\frac{1}{7}$ of 42 is 6, and 6 is contained in 12, 2 times. Therefore $\frac{4}{3}$ of 36 is $\frac{4}{9}$ of 9 times $\frac{2}{7}$ of 42.

4. $\frac{4}{3}$ of 36 is $\frac{4}{9}$ of 9 times 2 times what part of 42 ?

$\frac{4}{3}$ of 36 is $\frac{4}{9}$ of 9 times 2 times such a part of 42 as 42 is contained times in $\frac{1}{2}$ of $\frac{1}{9}$ of 9 times $\frac{1}{4}$ of 4 times $\frac{1}{3}$ of 36 ; $\frac{1}{3}$ of 36 is 12, and 4 times 12 is 48 ; $\frac{1}{4}$ of 48 is 12, and 9 times 12 is 108 ; $\frac{1}{9}$ of 108 is 12, and $\frac{1}{2}$ of 12 is 6 ; 42 is contained in 6, $\frac{6}{42}$ or $\frac{1}{7}$ times. Therefore $\frac{1}{3}$ of 36 is $\frac{4}{9}$ of 9 times 2 times $\frac{1}{7}$, or $\frac{2}{7}$, of 42.

5. $\frac{1}{3}$ of 36 is how many ninths of 9 times $\frac{2}{7}$ of 42 ?

$\frac{1}{3}$ of 36 is as many *ninths* of 9 times $\frac{2}{7}$ of 42, as $\frac{1}{9}$ of 9 times 2 times $\frac{1}{7}$ of 42 is contained times in 4 times $\frac{1}{3}$ of 36 ; $\frac{1}{3}$ of 36 is 12, and 4 times 12 is 48 ; $\frac{1}{7}$ of 42 is 6, and 2 times 6 is 12 ; 9 times 12 is 108, and $\frac{1}{9}$ of 108 is 12 ; 12 is contained in 48, 4 times. Therefore $\frac{1}{3}$ of 36 is $\frac{4}{9}$ of 9 times $\frac{2}{7}$ of 42.

6. $\frac{1}{3}$ of 36 is 4 times what part of 9 times $\frac{2}{7}$ of 42 ?

$\frac{1}{3}$ of 36 is 4 times such a part of 9 times $\frac{2}{7}$ of 42, as 9 times 2 times $\frac{1}{7}$ of 42 is contained times in $\frac{1}{4}$ of 4 times $\frac{1}{3}$ of 36 ; $\frac{1}{3}$ of 36 is 12, and 4 times 12 is 48 ; $\frac{1}{4}$ of 48 is 12 ; $\frac{1}{7}$ of 42 is 6, 2 times 6 is 12, and 9 times 12 is 108; 108 is contained in 12, $\frac{12}{108}$ or $\frac{1}{9}$ times. Therefore $\frac{1}{3}$ of 36 is 4 times, $\frac{1}{9}$ or $\frac{4}{9}$, of 9 times $\frac{2}{7}$ of 42.

7. $\frac{4}{9}$ of 9 times $\frac{2}{7}$ of 42 is $\frac{1}{3}$ of what number ?

$\frac{4}{9}$ of 9 times $\frac{2}{7}$ of 42 is $\frac{1}{3}$ of 3 times $\frac{1}{4}$ of 4 times $\frac{1}{9}$ of 9 times 2 times $\frac{1}{7}$ of 42. $\frac{1}{7}$ of 42 is 6, 2 times 6 is 12, and 9 times 12 is 108 ; $\frac{1}{9}$ of 108 is 12, and 4 times 12 is 48 ; $\frac{1}{4}$ of 48 is 12, and 3 times 12 is 36. Therefore $\frac{4}{9}$ of 9 times $\frac{2}{7}$ of 42 is $\frac{1}{3}$ of 36.

8. $\frac{4}{9}$ of 9 times $\frac{2}{7}$ of 42 is how many thirds of 36 ?

$\frac{4}{9}$ of 9 times $\frac{2}{7}$ of 42 is as many thirds of 36, as $\frac{1}{3}$ of 36 is contained times in 4 times $\frac{1}{9}$ of 9 times 2 times $\frac{1}{7}$ of 42 ; $\frac{1}{7}$ of 42 is 6, 2 times 6 is 12, and 9 times 12 is 108 ; $\frac{1}{9}$ of 108 is 12, and 4 times 12 is 48 ; $\frac{1}{3}$ of 36 is 12, and 12 is contained in 48, 4 times. Therefore $\frac{4}{9}$ of 9 times $\frac{2}{7}$ of 42 is $\frac{4}{3}$ of 36.

9. $\frac{4}{9}$ of 9 times $\frac{2}{7}$ of 42 is 4 times what part of 36 ?

$\frac{4}{9}$ of 9 times $\frac{2}{7}$ of 42 is 4 times such part of 36 as 36 is contained times in $\frac{1}{4}$ of 4 times $\frac{1}{9}$ of 9 times 2 times $\frac{1}{7}$ of 42 ; $\frac{1}{7}$ of 42 is 6, 2 times 6 is 12, and 9 times 12 is 108; $\frac{1}{9}$ of 108 is 12, and 4 times 12 is 48 ; $\frac{1}{4}$ of 48 is 12, and 36 is contained in 12, $\frac{12}{36}$ or $\frac{1}{3}$ times. Therefore $\frac{4}{9}$ of 9 times $\frac{2}{7}$ of 42 is 4 times, $\frac{1}{3}$ or $\frac{4}{3}$, of 36.

MULTIPLICATION TABLE.

Once	1	2	3	4	5	6
Twice	are 2	are 4	are 6	are 8	are 10	are 12
2 times	are 3	are 6	are 9	are 12	are 15	are 18
4 times	are 4	are 8	are 12	are 16	are 20	are 24
5 times	are 5	are 10	are 15	are 20	are 25	are 30
6 times	are 6	are 12	are 18	are 24	are 30	are 36
7 times	are 7	are 14	are 21	are 28	are 35	are 42
8 times	are 8	are 16	are 24	are 32	are 40	are 48
9 times	are 9	are 18	are 27	are 36	are 45	are 54
10 times	are 10	are 20	are 30	are 40	are 50	are 60
11 times	are 11	are 22	are 33	are 44	are 55	are 66
12 times	are 12	are 24	are 36	are 48	are 60	are 72

Once	7	8	9	10	11	12
Twice	are 14	are 16	are 18	are 20	are 22	are 24
3 times	are 21	are 24	are 27	are 30	are 33	are 36
4 times	are 28	are 32	are 36	are 40	are 44	are 48
5 times	are 35	are 40	are 45	are 50	are 55	are 60
6 times	are 42	are 48	are 54	are 60	are 66	are 72
7 times	are 49	are 56	are 63	are 70	are 77	are 84
8 times	are 56	are 64	are 72	are 80	are 88	are 96
9 times	are 63	are 72	are 81	are 90	are 99	are 108
10 times	are 70	are 80	are 90	are 100	are 110	are 120
11 times	are 77	are 88	are 99	are 110	are 121	are 132
12 times	are 84	are 96	are 108	are 120	are 132	are 144

	1	2	3	4	5	6
13 times	are 13	are 26	are 39	are 52	are 65	are 78
14 times	are 14	are 28	are 42	are 56	are 70	are 84
15 times	are 15	are 30	are 45	are 60	are 75	are 90
16 times	are 16	are 32	are 48	are 64	are 80	are 96
17 times	are 17	are 34	are 51	are 68	are 85	are 102
18 times	are 18	are 36	are 54	are 72	are 90	are 108
19 times	are 19	are 38	are 57	are 76	are 95	are 114
20 times	are 20	are 40	are 60	are 80	are 100	are 120
21 times	are 21	are 42	are 63	are 84	are 105	are 126
22 times	are 22	are 44	are 66	are 88	are 110	are 132
23 times	are 23	are 46	are 69	are 92	are 115	are 138
24 times	are 24	are 48	are 72	are 96	are 120	are 144
25 times	are 25	are 50	are 75	are 100	are 125	are 150

	7	8	9	10	11	12
13 times	are 91	are 104	are 117	are 130	are 143	are 156
14 times	are 98	are 112	are 126	are 140	are 154	are 168
15 times	are 105	are 120	are 135	are 150	are 165	are 180
16 times	are 112	are 128	are 144	are 160	are 176	are 192
17 times	are 119	are 136	are 153	are 170	are 187	are 204
18 times	are 126	are 144	are 162	are 180	are 198	are 216
19 times	are 133	are 152	are 171	are 190	are 209	are 228
20 times	are 140	are 160	are 180	are 200	are 220	are 240
21 times	are 147	are 168	are 189	are 210	are 231	are 252
22 times	are 154	are 176	are 198	are 220	are 242	are 264
23 times	are 161	are 184	are 207	are 230	are 253	are 276
24 times	are 168	are 192	are 216	are 240	are 264	are 288
25 times	are 175	are 200	are 225	are 250	are 275	are 300

	13	14	15	16	17	18
13 times	are 169	are 182	are 195	are 208	are 221	are 234
14 times	are 182	are 196	are 210	are 224	are 238	are 252
15 times	are 195	are 210	are 225	are 240	are 255	are 270
16 times	are 208	are 224	are 240	are 256	are 272	are 288
17 times	are 221	are 238	are 255	are 272	are 289	are 306
18 times	are 234	are 252	are 270	are 288	are 306	are 324
19 times	are 247	are 266	are 285	are 304	are 323	are 342
20 times	are 260	are 280	are 300	are 320	are 340	are 360
21 times	are 273	are 294	are 315	are 336	are 357	are 378
22 times	are 286	are 308	are 330	are 352	are 374	are 396
23 times	are 299	are 322	are 345	are 368	are 391	are 414
24 times	are 312	are 336	are 360	are 384	are 408	are 432
25 times	are 325	are 350	are 375	are 400	are 425	are 450

	19	20	21	22	23	24
13 times	are 247	are 260	are 273	are 286	are 299	are 312
14 times	are 266	are 280	are 294	are 308	are 322	are 336
15 times	are 285	are 30)	are 315	are 330	are 345	are 360
16 times	are 304	are 320	are 336	are 352	are 368	are 384
17 times	are 323	are 340	are 357	are 374	are 391	are 408
18 times	are 342	are 360	are 378	are 396	are 414	are 432
19 times	are 361	are 380	are 399	are 418	are 437	are 456
20 times	are 380	are 400	are 420	are 440	are 460	are 480
21 times	are 399	are 420	are 441	are 462	are 483	are 504
22 times	are 418	are 440	are 462	are 484	are 506	are 528
23 times	are 437	are 4 0	are 483	are 506	are 529	are 552
24 times	are 456	are 480	are 504	are 528	are 552	are 576
25 times	are 475	are 500	are 525	are 550	are 575	are 600

www.ingramcontent.com/pod-product-compliance
Lightning Source LLC
Chambersburg PA
CBHW030847270326
41928CB00007B/1258